The Yachtsman's Pilot
Skye and Northwest Scotland

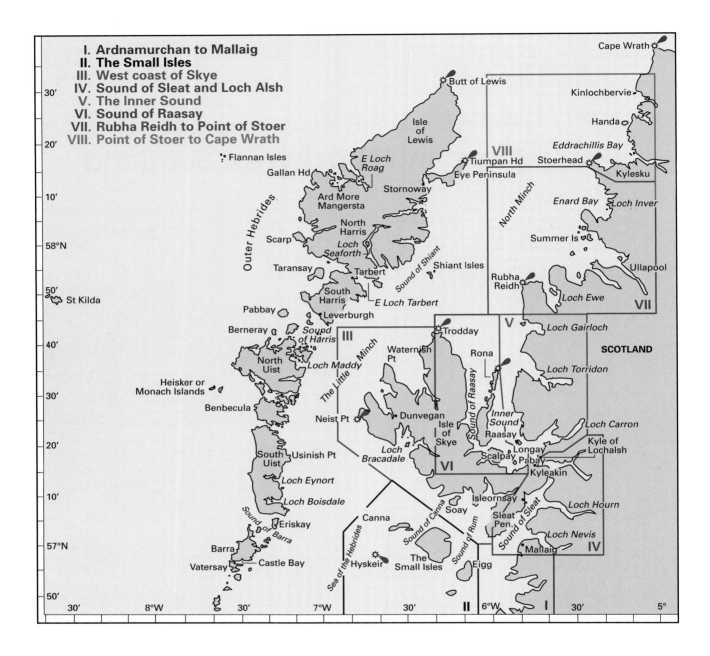

The Yachtsman's Pilot
Skye and
Northwest Scotland

MARTIN LAWRENCE

Imray Laurie Norie & Wilson

Published by
Imray Laurie Norie & Wilson Ltd
Wych House St Ives
Cambridgeshire PE27 5BT England
☎ +44 (0) 1480 462114 Fax +44 (0) 1480 496109
Email ilnw@imray.com
www.imray.com
2010

Martin Lawrence has asserted his right to be identified as the author of this work in
accordance with the Copyright, Designs and Patents Act 1988.

1st edition 1997
2nd edition 2002
3rd edition 2010

All photographs by the author unless otherwise credited.

ISBN 978 184623 178 0

British Library Cataloguing in Publication Data.
A catalogue record for this book is available from the British Library.

PLANS
The plans in this guide are not to be used for navigation. They are designed to
support the text and should at all times be used with navigational charts.

CAUTION
Every effort has been made to ensure the accuracy of this book. It contains selected
information and thus is not definitive and does not include all known information
on the subject in hand; this is particularly relevant to the plans, which should not be
used for navigation. The author believes that its selection is a useful aid to prudent
navigation, but the safety of a vessel depends ultimately on the judgement of the
navigator, who should assess all information, published or unpublished.

CORRECTIONS
The editors would be glad to receive any correc tions, information or suggestions
which readers may consider would improve the book, as new impressions will be
required from time to time. Letters should be addressed to the Editor, The
Yachtsman's Pilot – Skye and Northwest Scotland, care of the publishers. The more
pre cise the information the better, but even partial or doubtful information is
helpful, if it is made clear what the doubts are.

CORRECTIONAL SUPPLEMENTS
This pilot book will be amended at intervals by the issue of correctional
supplements. These are published on the internet at our website www.imray.com
and may be downloaded free of charge.

The last input of technical information was August 2010.

Printed in Singapore by Star Standard Industries Pte Ltd

Contents

Preface

The first volume of this series of *Yachtsman's Pilots* for the West Coast of Scotland was published 23 years ago. Renamed *Isle of Mull*, it is now in its fourth edition. The photos and plans of the new edition of this volume, *Skye and Northwest Scotland*, are printed in colour throughout, and I have taken many new aerial photos.

This is unlikely to be the first volume of the series to come to the reader's notice, so that its history need not be repeated here. While I have sailed on the West Coast for more than 30 years I make no claim to personal knowledge of every anchorage described, and my purpose is to gather information from every available source and present it in the clearest possible way. There are many people who know far more about individual areas than I do, and some of them have generously given me the benefit of their experience and taken a great deal of time to discuss their observations.

I do urge any yachtsman who knows of uncharted hazards or information which would be of value to other small boat users, to supply the fullest details to the Hydrographic Office. The Office relies heavily on information from users, particularly for less-frequented areas such as these, and is not sufficiently well funded to be able to update its surveys except for some very pressing commercial or military purpose.

The photographs used here have been chosen as far as possible to supplement the charts and plans. Ideally photos should be taken at low spring tides to reveal as many hazards as possible. Printing these photos in colour often shows more detail than is possible in monochrome. However, it takes many years to visit each place at a specific time of day and month, whether by sea, land or air – with no guarantee that conditions will be suitable for photography when one gets there, so that coverage isn't as comprehensive nor some of the photos not as clear as I would like. I have also used photos by other yachtsmen.

It is not always possible to present all relevant information on facing pages, and plans and photos should also be looked for on pages preceding and following the text.

Some people go to great lengths – or depths – to check uncharted rocks. Gillian Smith is standing on Bogha Stru in Loch Moidart North Channel, which is just covered, to provide a reference point for locating Bo Tony
Norman Smith

Acknowledgements

The staff of the Map Room of the National Library of Scotland have been patiently dealing with my requests for obscure information for many years.

I am particularly grateful to the following for information for this edition: Robert Arnold, Rob Teago, Philip Pendred, Norman and Gillian Smith, Tony Barry, Charles Barrington, Dick Fresson, John Macrae, John Shepherd, Tim Whittome, Robert Hollingdale, David Vass and Bob Bradfield.

The publishers are grateful to Elizabeth Cook who compiled the index.

Martin Lawrence,
Perth
2010

Author's note

Many of the plans in this book are based on British Admiralty charts with the permission of the Hydrographer of the Navy and the sanction of HM Stationery Office but, above and beyond that, I am extremely grateful to the Hydrographer and many of his staff who have taken time to search through archives and reply to requests for information.

There is much that is not fully known about parts of the West Coast and, in spite of checking by many people, it cannot be certain that all errors have been eliminated. The fact that an anchorage or passage is described is no guarantee that it is usable by you on the day you are there. There could well be hazards which I have missed by luck rather than good management and, in spite of all the efforts of Imray's staff and others, there may be simple errors which have been overlooked – even the supplements to the Admiralty *Pilot* contain the occasional comment 'for E read W'! Scepticism and checking against all other information available is the safest course to adopt … with any directions.

Before following the directions, plot the course on a large-scale chart and, if you are confident that any errors will not be fatal, proceed. If you disagree with what I have written, or find mistakes or changes, then please let me know through the publishers.

Martin Lawrence
Perth
2010

If you head north of Ardnamurchan, bear in mind that you have to make the return passage; *Thomasina* off Ardnamurchan   *Rinze van der Bij*

Introduction

The area described in this volume lies within a rectangle 100 miles by 50, equivalent to the English Channel between the Solent and the Straits of Dover, or the southern North Sea between Ramsgate and Cromer.

North of Ardnamurchan the scale of the landscape is, for the most part, more dramatic, and there are fewer of the intimate anchorages associated with the southern part of the west coast.

There are some extremely well-sheltered anchorages, but many of these will give you anxiousmoments before you are safely inside.

There are many islands, many inlets, no marinas(although one or two pontoons, now, have been established for visiting yachts), almost no commercial harbours, few services and supplies, and fewer organised entertainments, but the natives are friendly. Daylight in summer is longer than in the Channel, being 400–500 miles further north, and the weather is on the whole less settled. But if you are prepared for the conditions which this paragraph merely hints at, you may experience unique and memorable cruising. The whole area, however, is increasingly at risk from fish farming and future oil development and 'renewable' energy as well as pressure from visitors.

Over the last 10 years the number of visiting yachts in this area has grown enormously, with corresponding growth in the number of permanent moorings and visitors' moorings and, occasionally,landing pontoons.

Throughout the northwest highlands, Skye and other islands there is excellent climbing and hillwalking, and a small boat provides unique opportunities to combine climbing and sailing. Access to land: Rights of access open country throughout Scotland are defined in *The Access Code*, published by Scottish Natural Heritage, available from local Tourist Information Centres, and may also be downloaded from the internet at www.outdooraccess-scotland.com

This pilot sets out to provide as much information as may be useful to small-boat visitors to the waters of northwest Scotland, clearly and concisely. The upper limit of size for which the book is intended is a draught of 2m, and it includes information applicable to shoal-draught boats – centreboarders, trailer-sailers, twin-keel boats and multihulls, and motor cruisers. In many anchorages there are parts which are only accessible to shoal-draught boats, particularly those which can dry out fairly upright. However, while the smallest boats, even cruising dinghies, may be at home in much of the area described in this pilot, they must be soundly equipped and competently handled by experienced crews.

The West Coast is no place for anyone who is unable to deal with adverse conditions which may arise unexpectedly. A good way to gain experience of the West Coast is to take a berth on one of the skippered charter yachts or instructional courses which are available. Some of the waters covered by this volume are sheltered by islands or are within lochs which penetrate far among some of the highest hills in Britain. This shelter creates problems of its own, particularly the squalls which are generated in the lee of hills as well as the higher rainfall. Anyone who is capable of managing a yacht at a comparable distance from the shore whether in the North Sea, the Baltic, the English Channel, the Atlantic Coast of France or the Irish Sea should have little problem on the West Coast of Scotland. However, the lack of navigational marks (and the number of unmarked rocks) and the strong tides in some passages will require some adjustment on the part of the navigator. To set against these are the relative absence of commercial shipping, although timber is increasingly being transported by sea, using remote piers such as Dunvegan and Portree, and unusually large vessels may be met with in these areas. However visibility is usually good – except in rain; fog as such is fairly rare. To complete a round of generalisations, the climate is wetter and cooler than, for example, the south coast of England (although the further west you go, out of the lee of the hills, the drier the weather), but a compensating factor is the longer daylight in summer, so that you rarely need to sail at night.

Equipment should be as robust and reliable as for a yacht going a similar distance offshore anywhere in the English Channel or the North Sea, and a more comprehensive stock of spare parts carried, owing to the remoteness from sources of supply.

Anchors

So many yachts are now kept in marinas and only sail to another marina, or to a harbour, that anchoring is no longer an everyday operation but, on the West Coast, it is essential that the crew is thoroughly familiar with anchor handling. You should have at least two anchors, of the sizes recommended by anchor manufacturers or independent reference books, rather than those supplied as standard by boat builders which are often on the light side. Chain rather than rope will restrain a yacht from roving around in gusts, but if you do use rope it will help to have an 'angel' (a weight which can be let down to the seabed on a traveller). Whatever the design of the anchor there is no substitute for weight and I suspect that the reputation some anchorages have for poor holding may be rather more due to many yachts having inadequate anchors. Attention should be devoted to ease of handling – unless you stick to places with visitors' moorings (and there's no guarantee that one will be free) you will be using the anchor frequently.

Chartering

Charter boats are available, both for bareboat and skippered charters, within the area of this volume from Armadale in Skye and Badachro by Gairloch, as well as from further south. Many of the operators are members of Associated Scottish Yacht Charterers, whose brochure can be obtained from Sail Scotland, 11 Cairnbaan Cottages, Cairnbaan, Lochgilphead, Argyll, PA31 8SJ *Email* info@sailscotland.co.uk. General tourist information may be had from the VisitScotland, Level 3, Ocean Point 1, 94 Ocean Drive, Edinburgh EH6 6JH ① 0845 22 55 121. *Email* info@visitscotland.com.

Charts

Imray's charts C65–C67 at 1:150,000 give better coverage for passage making than any current Admiralty charts and are more convenient to use.

Betwen Ardnamurchan and the north of Skye and Loch Gairloch the four Admiralty charts 2207–2210 (1:50,000) are essential. There are no larger-scale charts between Ardnamurchan and Mallaig and the south side of Skye. Further north, the scale of chart which you choose depends on the degree of intricate pilotage in which you intend to indulge. Probably you will need some larger-scale charts (around 1:25,000) together with either the Imray charts or Admiralty charts *1785*, *1794* and *1795* at 1:100,000.

Get your charts early so that you have time to order more if it looks as though your first choice is not enough.

The horizontal datum of Admiralty charts covering the area referred to in this volume is in the process of being changed. The difference in most cases is less than 100m, which is enough to miss the entrance of a harbour in poor visibility, or to fail to avoid concealed hazards, especially if the navigator is putting undue faith in the precision of electronic position fixing.

Climbing combines naturally with cruising in northwest Scotland

The newer charts are clearly marked WGS84, and editions of charts using this datum began to appear from September 2000.

On some GPS receivers the appropriate datum can be selected; that used by default is WGS84, but the older datum, OSGB36, may not always be identified on the chart. This is also the datum for Ordnance Survey maps.

If you have a chart with an unidentified datum and a GPS receiver on which the datum cannot be selected, allow at least 100m margin. Take an early opportunity to calibrate your GPS with a known charted object. Within the area covered by this pilot the shift from the position given by GPS receivers calibrated to WGS84 to charts set out to OSGB36 varies between 0·0 and 0·01 minutes northward and between 0·06 and 0·08 minutes eastward.

Some obsolete charts show more detail than any current one and sometimes at a larger scale, but the soundings are in feet and fathoms. They should of course only be used to supplement current charts, not as a substitute for them; although it has been observed that 'rocks don't move', new hazards are discovered (sometimes the hard way), buoys are moved around, and new features are constructed.

Maps published by Ordnance Survey at 1:25,000 and 1:50,000 provide more topographical detail than current hydrographic charts (*see Appendix II*). Where the charts are at a small scale the Ordnance Survey maps may also be some help for navigation. Ordnance Survey maps at 1:25,000 are occasionally useful where there is no Admiralty chart at a sufficiently large scale. These carry the brand name *Explorer*, and an index sheet of all OS maps is available from larger bookshops, Imrays and from Ordnance Survey, Romsey Road, Southampton SO16 4GU ① 08456 050505

www.ordnancesurvey.co.uk

The current edition of the publication *Welcome Anchorages*, available free of charge from marinas and chandlers throughout the West Coast, provides details of facilities provided at each harbour.

A full set of Admiralty charts, as well as Imray charts, for the west coast of Scotland is available on disc. These can be read with any modern laptop computer able to read a CD, and can be linked to a GPS attachment. It is obviously essential to carry an adequate set of paper charts, in case any link in the technological chain fails.

New, very precise, surveys are being carried out throughout the west coast of Scotland by Antares Charts. These surveys are intended to be used with electronic plotters or with a laptop computer with a simple (and modestly-priced) GPS accessory. For full details including current and intended future output go to www.antarescharts.co.uk.

Travel

There are good roads to those places on the mainland coast where one might make crew changes, although they are often narrow and patience needs to be exercised with touring coaches, caravans and heavy lorries.

Car ferries to Skye run from Mallaig to Armadale and the new bridge from Kyle of Lochalsh to Skye for which the tolls have been abolished.

Trains to Mallaig run from Glasgow via Fort William, and to Kyle of Lochalsh from Inverness. A variety of long-distance and local bus services reach most places eventually.

Trailed boats may be launched at Arisaig, which is a few miles south of Mallaig, Plockton, Gairloch, Kylesku and, for Arisaig, phone Arisaig Marine ☎ 01687 450224; the others are public facilities. For train information ☎ 08457 484950, for bus information ☎ 08705 505050. There are no air services to any part of the coast in this book, but airstrips at Plockton and Broadford are usable by light aircraft.

If recovering a car from further south a convenient staging point is Dunstaffnage Marina, which can be reached by a combination of bus and train from Mallaig or Kyle. Make prior arrangements with management at Dunstaffnage ☎ 01631 566555.

Passage making

Unless you are crossing the Minch the distance between the entrances of sheltered anchorages is rarely more than 12 miles.

Serious navigation is still necessary but, for much of the time, it is a matter of pilotage by eye and satisfying yourself that what you see corresponds to the chart.

The most useful position lines are transits such as tangents of islands, or beacons in line with headlands and these should be picked out on the chart in advance.

Compass bearings should, of course, be taken as well, if only to avoid wrongly identifying a whole group of islands.

At night salient points and hazards in the Minches, Sound of Sleat and Inner Sound, and in the approaches to lochs and inlets used by naval and commercial traffic, are well enough lit but in these latitudes there is little darkness in the summer months.

Radiobeacons are located at Stornoway (aero), Butt of Lewis and Cape Wrath. Details are given in the appropriate chapters.

Visibility is commonly good and fog as such is rare. The Admiralty Pilot says that 'visibility of less than ½ mile may reach three days per month in midsummer' and visibility of less than two miles 'does not average more than three days per month during the worst summer weather at Stornoway and Tiree'.

Lobster and prawn creel floats are often encountered even in the middle of the Minch and in the fairway of approaches to anchorages. Often, floating lines lie upstream of the float, especially at low tide, and sometimes stray lines lie downstream.

Weather

Weather is extremely variable and any statistics can be interpreted so widely as to be of little help. After visibility the aspects of most concern are wind speed and direction, and rainfall.

Rainfall is greatly affected by the proximity to high ground, and annual figures vary from less than 1,000mm at Arisaig to between 1,250 and 1,800mm in the Sound of Sleat and Inner Sound, and between 2,300 and 3,000mm at the heads of Lochs Hourn, Nevis and Torridon.

Broadcast forecasting schedules vary from year to year and a current almanac should be consulted. Apart from the shipping forecasts on BBC Radio 4 and inshore waters forecasts on Radio 3, general weather forecasts are often equally relevant where land and sea are so much intermingled.

Inshore weather forecasts are broadcast from Stornoway Coastguard on VHF R/T on different channels depending on the location of the transmitting beacon, after an initial announcement on Ch 16 at, or shortly after the following times:

Stornoway Clyde

0110, 0210 New Inshore Forecast plus previous Outlook, Gale Warnings.

0410, 0510 Repetition as per previous Schedule A or B broadcast plus new SWW*.

0710, 0810 Full Maritime Safety Information broadcast, including new Inshore Forecast and Outlook, Gale Warnings, Shipping Forecast, Navigation Warnings, UBFACTS and GUNFACTS where appropriate, 3-Day Fisherman's Forecast when and where appropriate.

1010, 1110 Repetition as per previous Schedule A or B broadcast plus new SWW*.

1310, 1410 New Inshore Forecast plus previous Outlook, Gale Warnings.

1610, 1710 Repetition as per previous Schedule A or B broadcast plus new SWW*.

1910, 2010 As 0710, 0810

2210, 2310 Repetition as per Schedule Gale Warnings broadcast plus new SWW*.

* SWW = Strong Wind Warning

Aerials and Frequencies

Barra –10, Melvaig, Forsnaval, Arisaig –23, Skriag, Clettravel, Portnaguran –84, Butt of Lewis, Drumfearn, Rodel –86

MF Butt of Lewis 1743kHz: Inshore Forecast / WZ Ardnamurchan Point to Cape Wrath

Shipping / GW Areas Hebrides, Bailey, Rockall, Faeroes, Fair Isle, SE Iceland, Malin Additional 3-Day Fisherman's Forecast (October–March) GUNFACTS and SUBFACTS

In some locations (e.g. Loch Nevis, Soay, Loch Scavaig) the initial announcement may be heard but not the subsequent broadcast.

MetFax services may be obtained from hotels which cater for yachtsmen, and from harbourmasters.

Tides

The spring range throughout the area is about 4·5m, and neaps about 1·5m. Tidal streams are strong wherever the movement of a large body of water is constricted by narrows, and there are often overfalls at the seaward end of narrow passages, particularly with wind against tide. Overfalls also occur off many headlands, and eddies are formed, usually downtide of a promontory or islet or even a submerged reef, but sometimes in a bay uptide of the obstruction. There are also usually overfalls wherever two tidal streams meet.

Anchorages

A few very general observations may be helpful. Steep high ground to windward is unlikely to provide good shelter – in fresh winds there may be turbulent gusts on its lee side, or the wind may be deflected to blow from a completely different direction, or funnel down a valley. After a hot windless day there may be a strong katabatic wind down the slope, usually in the early morning – such conditions are by no means unknown in Scotland. Trees to windward will absorb a lot of wind and provide good shelter.

Within some anchorages there are often several suitable berths depending on conditions and it may not be practicable to describe them all, nor to mark each one on the plans. In any case, an anchorage suitable for a shoal-draught boat 6m long may be inaccessible to a 15m yacht with a draught of 2m, and a berth which would give shelter for the larger yacht might be uncomfortably exposed for the smaller.

Rivers, burns and streams generally carry down debris, often leaving a shallow or drying bank of stones, sand or silt, over which the unwary may swing – frequently in the middle of the night. The heads of lochs and inlets commonly dry off for more than ½ mile.

Within any anchorage the quality of the bottom may vary greatly. Mud is common (usually where there is little current), but its density may not be consistent and there are likely to be patches of rock, boulders and stones; also clay which tends to break out suddenly. Sand is also common, but sometimes it is so hard that an anchor, particularly a light one, will not dig in. Weed of all kinds appears to be on the increase, but it does vary from year to year.

Increasingly, moorings for yachts and fishing and other workboats, as well as fish farms, are being laid within esablished anchorages, preventing or restricting their use. Preservation of anchorages is one of the main functions of the West Highland Anchorages and Moorings Association (WHAM), who would like to hear about any unauthorised obstruction. The Hon. Secretary of WHAM is David Vass 33 Ochlochy Park, Dunblane, FK15 0DX ☎ 01786 822840.

Fish farms are increasing at an alarming rate, usually outwith the most popular places, but attempts are sometimes made to establish them in recognised anchorages as well. There are two main forms: cages for 'fin fish', (usually salmon), and rows of buoys from which ropes are suspended, on which shellfish are 'grown'. These buoys may have ropes between them on or close to the surface. Fish cages may be moved around within a bay or inlet, often because they have created so much pollution that the fish can no longer live in the original location, so that they may not be found where shown on a chart or plan. The boundary of an area licensed for fish farming is sometimes marked by buoys, usually yellow and sometimes lit. These are often a long way from the cages, and there may or may not be moorings or other obstructions within the area marked out by the buoys.

Beacons are often not at the extreme end of the hazard which they mark.

Fish farms are a universal hazard and a source of pollution

Car ferries run to very tight schedules and the space to manoeuvre at a ferry terminal is often restricted. Yachts must leave clear turning space near ferry terminals; apart from the safety aspect they may be disturbed by the wash from a ferry's bow thruster. Ferry schedules differ from day to day, and Caledonian MacBrayne's current timetable (easily obtained from tourist offices and ferry offices or by post from Caledonian MacBrayne Ltd, The Ferry Terminal, Gourock PA19 1QP, ☎ 01475 650100 www.calmac.co.uk) is useful to avoid conflict in the often very constricted space around terminals.

Moorings for fishing boats are laid in many anchorages, but many are not used in summer as their owners are often working on the Atlantic coast of the Outer Hebrides, and you may be invited to use a fisherman's mooring. Do not pick up a buoy unless you are sure that it is a mooring buoy and not marking creels for storing live prawns – or another yacht's anchor buoy!

Visitors' moorings are provided by local hotels free of charge to yachts whose crews patronise their establishments, as well as by HIE (Highlands and Islands Enterprise, formerly Highlands and Islands Development Board). They are arranged (as they have to be) to suit the largest boats likely to use them, and a boat on a mooring behaves differently from a boat at anchor. The effect is often to reduce rather than increase the number of visiting boats which can use an anchorage. There is no guarantee that the mooring is suitable for any boat intending to use it.

Visitors' moorings have been laid in several locations to attract more business to local traders. These moorings have large blue buoys marked 'visitors 15 tons'. There is no pick-up, and a rope has to be fed through a ring on top of the buoy. If your bow is so high that the buoy is out of reach and you cannot pass your rope through the ring, the best way to secure to one of these moorings is to lead a rope from the bow to the lowest point amidships, pick up the buoy there and take the end of the rope back to the bow. Two turns should be taken round the ring, and an appropriate knot formed to avoid the chafe which would occur with a slip rope.

The practice of rafting up together on these moorings is not now encouraged.

The provision of visitors moorings throughout the West Coast is under review, and the co-ordination of improved facilities throughout Highland region is the responsibility of the harbourmaster at Kyle, who welcomes comments and queries from users (☎ 01599 534167).

Quays, piers, jetties, slips, linkspans and related structures are in need of some definition, as the categories overlap and a structure identified on the chart may have fallen into disuse, or been replaced by one of a different type, or have a description well above its status. The following definitions are used in this book, to give some indication of what you may expect to find.

A quay, wharf or pier is used by fishing boats and occasional coasters, and usually has at least 2m of water at its head at chart datum. It is often constructed of piles or open framing, or stone or concrete with vertical timber fendering, alongside which it is difficult for a small yacht to lie without a robust fender board. A pier projects from the shore, but a quay or wharf is either part of a harbour or parallel to the shore. Many of these structures were erected or extended by the Admiralty 40–50 years ago and some which have not been maintained are in very poor condition.

Ferry terminals all have a linkspan for a bow-loading car ferry. The inner end is hinged and the outer end, supported between concrete towers, is raised or lowered to match the height of the ramp on the ferry, according to the state of the tide. The linkspan is usually at one end of a quay alongside which the ferry lies.

A jetty is smaller and, for yachts, more user-friendly but often dries alongside. Newer jetties are constructed of more or less smooth concrete, older ones of stone, often with a very uneven surface; a few are of timber.

A slip runs down at an angle into the water, although its outer end may be above water at low tide and it may be used by a ferry to an inshore island. There is sometimes sufficient depth for a yacht to go alongside a slip for a brief visit ashore for stores.

With the enormous growth in inshore fishing and fish-farming many of these structures are in regular use by fishermen whose livelihood depends on being able to land their produce quickly, and yachts should take care not to obstruct them.

Dues are charged at some piers and harbours, even for a brief visit to take on water. While this may be seen as a way in which yachtsmen can contribute to the local economy, the charges sometimes appear disproportionate to the service obtained. The Highland Council offer a sort of 'season ticket' for a yacht to use two or several of their piers or harbours over a period of time. This arrangement does not apply to Arisaig, Mallaig, Ullapool, or any other harbours not owned by Highland Council.

Access to Lighthouse sites the Northern Lighthouse Board operates a number of lighthouses with adjacent boat landings. Since the departure of lightkeepers from these sites, the landings are no longer maintained and NLB accepts no liability for injuries or damage caused by unauthorised access to these sites.

mSACs

The following note about marine Special Areas of Conservation has been provided by WHAM and Scottish Natural Heritage. There are currently four mSACs within the area covered by this volume, in the Sound of Arisaig, Lochs Duich, Long and Alsh, Ascrib Islands, and Loch Laxford.

Those who engage in boating and recreational diving on the west coast benefit from the many small harbours and anchorages and the unspoiled environment. We tend to take much of this for granted, but it is in everyone's interest that this environment is protected so that future generations can continue to enjoy it.

Under the European Habitats Directive the UK Government has agreed to identify a network of protected marine areas around our coasts to safeguard important species and their habitats. Around seventy sites have been identified around the UK and of these around two dozen are on the west coast of Scotland. For some of these sites, including Loch Maddy and the Sound of Arisaig, management committees have been established, including representatives from all local interest groups. Scottish Natural Heritage, Silvan House, 3rd Floor East, 231 Corstorphine Road, Edinburgh, EH12 7AT ✆ 0131 316 2600 www.snh.gov.uk produces excellent leaflets giving details of the special features of the mSACs. In addition, on land adjacent to some sites areas of Special Scientific Interest (SSSIs) are being designated.

There is no intention to try to restrict access to mSAC or to SSSIs; indeed, that would be counterproductive as the aim is to make everyone aware of the special features of the sites so that they can be appreciated by visitors. In a few cases and by mutual agreement some types of fishing are being discouraged because of damage which may be caused to sea life on the bottom; in future in a few mSAC boat owners may be encouraged to anchor only in recognised anchorages for the same reason, an anchor and chain can cause considerable damage as it sweeps the bottom due to the action of tide and wind.

Facilities

Considerable time, resourcefulness and imagination need to be devoted to obtaining supplies or services but local people are, as it were, in the same boat and usually go out of their way to be helpful. Ferrymen, piermasters, hotel keepers, postmistresses and fishermen are all willing and useful sources of information, and there are many services and sources of supply that are too irregular or ephemeral or unknown to be listed here.

There are few yachting services as such, although yacht chandlers at Badachro, Ullapool and Portree will advise.

Caley Marina at Inverness, ✆ 01463 233437, *Email* info@caleymarina.com operates a mobile repair service.

Sailing clubs exist at Plockton, Gairloch and Ullapool.

Showers or baths are often available at hotels.

Mobile banks operate throughout the Highlands and Islands.

Diesel is often more easily available by hose in small fishing harbours, but do not expect quick service: fuel is supplied to yachts as a favour, although usually very willingly, but the person dispensing it may have better things to do than turn out to supply a relatively small quantity.

Water supplies at the quayside are fairly rare, and a yacht with built-in tanks should have a portable container or two, together with a straight-sided funnel, with which to fill the tank. A 20-metre hose of the flat variety on a reel, with a universal coupling to fit on any sort of tap is also well worth carrying, as several small jetties have taps but no hoses. These small jetties, although they may only be approachable above half tide, are usually more convenient than the massive piled ferry piers, where the only hose may be too large to serve a yacht.

Eating ashore A reasonably varied selection of eating places is scattered throughout the area, one or two aspiring to gourmet status, and many at which you will eat well if unadventurously, whether in a restaurant or a bar. No recommendations are made as establishments can change hands, and standards, rapidly.

Communications

Phone boxes are fairly well distributed and are referred to where known, but the 'rationalisation' of the telephone service may lead to a reduction in their numbers.

Post offices Many now have very restricted hours of opening.

VHF radiotelephones The mountainous nature of this coast puts some areas out of range of coastguard transmitters and mobile phones.

Emergencies

Serious and immediate emergencies (including medical ones) are usually best referred to the coastguard. If you don't have VHF R/T but are able to get ashore (for example, if a crew member is ill), phone the coastguard or police. For less serious problems, such as a mechanical breakdown out of range of a boatyard, mechanics experienced at least with tractor or fishing-boat engines, will often be found locally.

Coastguard The Maritime Rescue Sub-Centres for the area are at Clyde ✆ 01475 729988 and Stornoway ✆ 01851 702013.

Lifeboats are stationed, within the limits of this volume, at Mallaig and Loch Inver and, further afield, at Oban, Castlebay, Stornoway and Tobermory.

Notes on plans and pilotage directions

Generally the conventions used on Admiralty charts have been followed so that this pilot may be used in conjunction with them. See also *Charts* on page 3.

In each chapter, information about charts, tides, dangers and marks, relevant to the whole, comes first; then any passage directions, sometimes including certain anchorages where it is necessary to relate these to plans associated with the passages; then any branches from the main passage; and

INTRODUCTION

KEY TO SYMBOLS ON PLANS

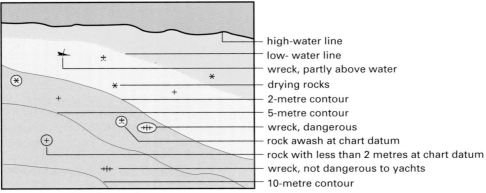

- high-water line
- low- water line
- wreck, partly above water
- drying rocks
- 2-metre contour
- 5-metre contour
- wreck, dangerous
- rock awash at chart datum
- rock with less than 2 metres at chart datum
- wreck, not dangerous to yachts
- 10-metre contour

All depths and heights are in metres

finally individual anchorages, usually in the same sequence as the passages described.

Conspicuous features are listed to help identification in poor visibility.

Lights, and any directions for making a passage or approach by night, are listed separated from the description of dangers and marks, as most of us sail mainly by day, and this reduces the amount of information to be absorbed.

Bearings are from seaward and refer to true north. A few of the plans are not orientated with north at the top in order to make the best use of the space available, but reference to the north point on the plan will make this clear.

Distances are given in nautical miles and cables (tenths of a nautical mile); a distance of less than q cable is generally expressed in metres.

Co-ordinates to locate anchorages are approximate – not waypoints, for entrance. Waypoints, specifically, are indicated by the standard symbol.

Depths and heights are given in metres to correspond with current Admiralty charts.

Depths are related to the current chart datum which is generally lower than that on older charts. It is the lowest level to which the surface of the sea is expected to fall owing to astronomical causes. If high barometric pressure and/or strong offshore winds coincide with a low spring tide the water may fall below this level, in which case there will be less depth than shown on the chart or sketch plan.

Tides Heights of tides are represented by five sets of figures; these are: mean high water springs (MHWS), mean high water neaps (MHWN), mean tide level (MTL), mean low water neaps (MLWN), mean low water springs (MLWS).

The word 'mean' is important because (for example) low water springs in any particular fortnight may be substantially higher or lower than the mean.

If you have tide tables which give heights of tides at Ullapool you will be able to relate the tide on any particular day to the equivalent figures there (5·2, 3·9, 3·0, 2·1, 0·7) and judge whether the rise and fall will be greater or less than the mean.

The difference between times of tides at Ullapool and Dover may vary by as much as 40 minutes, so that tide tables for Ullapool will give more accurate results than those for Dover. Tide tables for Ullapool are included in all almanacs but are not published separately; but the constant for that port is +0110 relative to Oban, for which a booklet of tables is widely available.

Shelter The heading 'Shelter' at the beginning of each chapter implies an anchorage for which to run in reasonable visibility if the wind is increasing.

Place names are a frequent source of confusion and there may be differences between the name used on a current chart, on an older chart, by local people and by yachtsmen. Anglicisations or translations are sometimes used quite arbitrarily on current charts among a nest of Gaelic names. The name on the current chart (or in the absence of a name on the chart, the OS map) is always given in this pilot, together with a popular name if the chart name is unpronounceable.

As place names often need to be spoken the following approximate pronunciation of common words in names may be helpful:

Bagh Bay
Bogha Bo'
Caol Kyle
Caolas Kyles
Dubh Doo
Mhor Vore
Rubha Ru'

Names of lochs, etc, are normally written as two words (Loch Inver, for example), but the name of a settlement beside the loch as a single word (Lochinver).

Photographs and views from sea level are used to illustrate transits and clearing marks, or to help identify landmarks, while air and hilltop photos often show more detail than can be included in the plans. Transits are, in some cases, more clearly illustrated when the marks used are not actually aligned; where this is done the marks are indicated by pointers.

I. Ardnamurchan to Mallaig

It used to be customary for any yacht returning from a cruise beyond Ardnamurchan to display a bunch of heather at the end of her bowsprit as a token of having been round this exposed headland.

Ardnamurchan is a key point in any cruise on the west coast, partly because of the exposure, but mainly by contrast with the sheltered waters of the Sound of Mull.

The Point itself has none of the hazards associated with such headlands as Portland Bill or Land's End; there are no off-lying rocks or shoals, nor strong tides, but the bottom is uneven and beating against such tide as there is can be very unpleasant.

As the prevailing wind is from the southwest these conditions are most likely to arise on your way home, and the possibility should be allowed for in planning a cruise.

For the Small Isles see Chapter II.

After a yacht has rounded Ardnamurchan the passage north-northeast gradually takes her into more sheltered water towards the Sound of Sleat, but rocks both marked and unmarked lie as much as a couple of miles offshore.

Tidal streams run at up to 4kns in places with relatively shoal banks which can cause an unpleasant sea. Most of the lochs between Ardnamurchan and Mallaig are difficult to find the way into, but some of them are outstandingly attractive and well worth the effort.

The north side of the Ardnamurchan peninsula has no shelter, except in moderate offshore winds in Loch Ceann Traigh (Kentra) at its east end, and there are several dangerous rocks along this shore.

Loch Moidart, between the Ardnamurchan peninsula and the major inlet of the Sound of Arisaig, is very difficult to enter.

The Sound of Arisaig itself divides into Loch Ailort and Loch nan Uamh, both of which involve intricate pilotage, but in the mouth of Loch Ailort there is an island behind which it is feasible to run for shelter given reasonable visibility.

North of Rubh' Arisaig on the north side of the Sound of Arisaig is Loch nan Ceall (Arisaig Harbour), entrance to which would be almost impossible without the beacons erected by the yacht centre there. Note that Arisaig Harbour and the Sound of Arisaig are entirely separate places.

Mallaig, towards the entrance of the Sound of Sleat, is a busy fishing and ferry harbour, fairly easily entered by day or night, good for supplies. A new basin has been built to the north, but is often unusable, so that the harbour is often congested. Visitors moorings are available.

Charts

The only relevant Admiralty chart is *2207* at a scale of 1:50,000, but its northern margin falls a mile short of Mallaig. Chart *2208* will probably be needed for the continuation northward in any case. Imray's chart *C65* extends to Mallaig.

Tides

Off Ardnamurchan, the flood stream runs northeastwards, and the spring rate is 1½ knots. On the ebb an eddy sets inshore south of the point. Heavy seas build up with onshore winds, especially with wind against tide, and it is best to keep two miles off the point.

Between Eigg and the mainland tidal streams run as follows:

The northeast-going stream begins +0550 Ullapool (+0130 Dover)

The southwest-going stream begins −0010 Ullapool (−0430 Dover).

The maximum rate is generally 1kn but, near the east shore of Eigg, the rate is up to 4kns; in the bight between the north side of Ardnamurchan and Rubh' Arisaig the rate is negligible.

Dangers and marks

The lighthouse at Ardnamurchan is very conspicuous but, if approaching from the Sound of Mull, it is not visible until it bears 001°.

Bo Kora Ben, a submerged rock with a least depth of 1·8m, lies six cables north-northeast of Ardnamurchan lighthouse and two cables offshore.

Bo Faskadale, a group of drying and submerged rocks six miles northeast of Ardnamurchan lighthouse and more than two miles offshore, is marked on its northwest side by a green conical light buoy which is often difficult to identify if there is any sea running.

The only other artificial mark is the white light beacon on Eilean Chathastail at the southeast point of Eigg.

Off the Arisaig promontory, on the mainland east of Eigg, rocks above water and drying extend more than half a mile from the shore and, further north, many drying rocks lie more than a mile from the shore.

Several banks, although more than 14m below chart datum, cause very heavy seas, particularly with wind against tide.

The two most significant are Maxwell Bank, about a mile across, one mile southeast of Eigg, and Oberon Bank which is small in extent, three miles east of the point of Eigg.

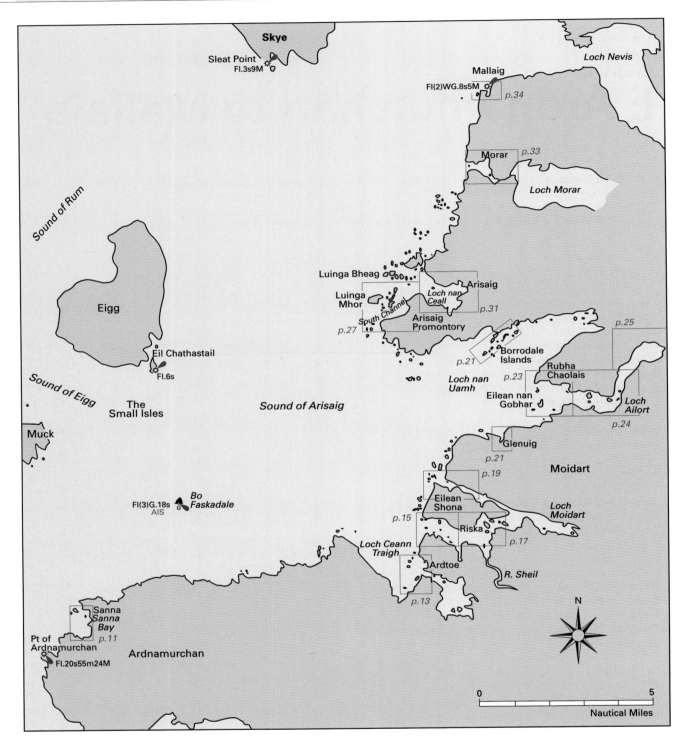

Skye

Sleat Point
Fl.3s9M

Loch Nevis

Mallaig
Fl(2)WG.8s5M *p.34*

Morar *p.33*

Loch Morar

Sound of Rum

Eigg

Luinga Bheag

Luinga Mhor

Loch nan Ceall

Arisaig

p.31

South Channel *p.27*

Arisaig Promontory

p.21

p.25

Eil Chathastail
Fl.6s

Borrodale Islands

Rubha Chaolais

p.23

Loch nan Uamh

Eilean nan Gobhar

Loch Ailort

p.24

Sound of Eigg

The Small Isles

Sound of Arisaig

Glenuig

p.21

Muck

p.19

Moidart

Bo Faskadale
Fl(3)G.18s
AIS

Eilean Shona

p.15

Riska

Loch Moidart

p.17

Loch Ceann Traigh

Ardtoe

R. Sheil

p.13

N

Sanna
Sanna Bay
p.11

Pt of Ardnamurchan
Fl.20s55m24M

Ardnamurchan

0   5

Nautical Miles

Rum
Muck

Skye

Eigg

Ardnamurchan

A local magnetic anomaly is charted east of Muck and south of Eigg. Another has been noted two miles south of Muck.

Passage notes

⊕ Two miles west of Ardnamurchan 56°43'·5N 6°17'W
⊕ ¼ mile northwest of Bo Faskadale 56°47'·7N 6°17'·0W

The passage from Ardnamurchan north-northeast towards the Sound of Sleat is straightforward enough in clear, moderate weather.

From a point two miles off Ardnamurchan steer 037° to pass east of Eigg.

To avoid Maxwell Bank, alter course more to the east, not less than 070°, when Bo Faskadale buoy has been identified, or when the southwest side of Rum comes open north of Muck bearing 322°.

Heading south or southwest, particularly from Arisaig, tend towards Muck and Eigg until Bo Faskadale buoy is identified.

North side of Ardnamurchan

⊕ ¼ mile north of Sgeir Charrach 56°47'·7N 5°57'·5W

The passage along the north side of Ardnamurchan has two dangers which are fairly easily avoided although there are no specific clearing marks.

Elizabeth Rock with a least depth of 0·7m, lies one mile south of Bo Faskadale buoy and 1¼ miles offshore.

Sgeir Charrach which dries 2·6m (at approximately half-tide), lies ¼ mile off Rubha Aird Druimnich which is the most northerly point on the peninsula.

Sgeir Carrach generally breaks, even at high water. Bo Ruadh, about four cables east-southeast of Sgeir Charrach, may be a hazard especially when sailing from east.

Soundings are very irregular here and give no guide to position. Steer to keep Rubha Aird Druimnich bearing 083° until Bo Faskadale buoy is abaft the beam, then steer to keep the south point of the Sound of Arisaig, Rubh' a' Phuill Bhig, bearing not less than 060°, to clear Sgeir Charrach.

Lights

At night the following lights (in clear weather, as they are a long way apart) make a direct passage between Ardnamurchan and the Sound of Sleat reasonably straightforward.

Ardnamurchan lighthouse Fl.20s55m24M
Eilean Chathastail, southeast of Eigg, Fl.6s24m8M
Bo Faskadale buoy Fl(3)G.18s
Sleat Point light beacon Fl.3s20m9M

The harbour at Mallaig is well lit, but there are no lights at any other anchorage.

Anchorages

Sanna Bay

⊕ South of Sgeir Horsgate 56°44'·6N 6°12'W

A delightful sandy bay 1½ miles northeast of Ardnamurchan lighthouse, sheltered to some extent by a reef projecting from its southwest side, Sanna Bay should probably be treated as only an occasional anchorage.

From the south the bay immediately north of the lighthouse might be mistaken for Sanna Bay and from the north, White Sand Bay, which lies east of Sanna Point, might be taken for it.

Meall Sanna behind Sanna Bay is the highest land on this part of the coast; apart from this the bay can only be identified by reference to the lighthouse and Sanna Point, north of which the coast falls away to the east.

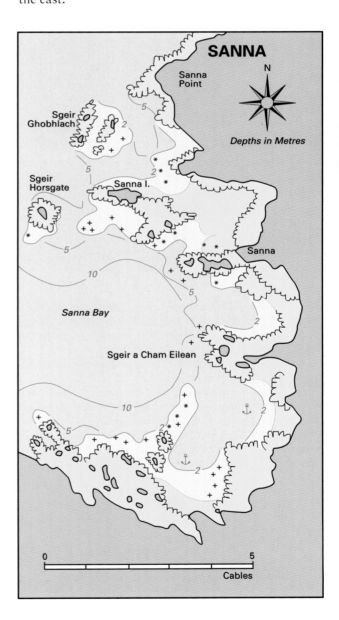

Opposite The Small Isles come into view as Ardnamurchan is opened up

I. ARDNAMURCHAN TO MALLAIG

Sanna Bay and the Small Isles. Some protection is provided by the drying reef in the centre left foreground

Tides

Constant at Loch Moidart –0048 Ullapool
(–0508 Dover)

Height in metres at Loch Moidart

MHWS	MHWN	MTL	MLWN	MLWS
4·8	3·5	2·6	1·6	0·5

Dangers

Bo Kora Ben, a submerged rock, 1·8m, lies halfway between the lighthouse and the south point of Sanna Bay, two cables off the north point of the bay to the south of Sanna Bay.

To the north of Sanna Bay drying rocks extend ¼ mile west-southwest of Sanna Point.

A reef, parts of which dry, extends at least two-thirds of the way across the mouth of the southeast part of the bay from its southwest side.

Even on the quietest day there is often a swell running into the bay, and the marks by which to avoid the reef are not easy to identify.

Approach and anchorages

From south keep at least ¼ mile offshore until Sanna Bay is well open, to avoid Bo Kora Ben.

Steer towards Sgeir Horsgate on the north side of the bay and approach as from the north (see below) to be sure of avoiding the reef.

From north pass at least ¼ mile off Sanna Point, and southwest of Sgeir Horsgate.

Steer for the more southerly of two white sandy beaches ahead, below the south peak of Meall Sanna, bearing 110° to 120° (depending on how close you are to Sgeir Horsgate).

Pass about ½ cable south of the rocky peninsula, Sgeir a' Cham Eilean, and for a short visit if there is little swell, anchor off the beach ahead.

To reach the inner anchorage, when about two-thirds of the way along the detached part of Sgeir a' Cham Eilean, turn to head about 204° towards a detached white cottage on the southeast shore with a stone barn to the left of it.

On a clear day the view over the Small Isles from Meall Sanna will make the climb well worthwhile.

Supplies

No supplies. Phone box at south side of the bay.

↓ Meall Sanna

↑ Sgeir a' Cham Eilean

Loch Ceann Traigh (Kentra)

A bay 1½ miles wide and 1½ miles deep at the east end of the Ardnamurchan peninsula, open to the north but providing occasional anchorage in offshore winds off sandy beaches at the south end. Fish cages are moored at the head of the bay.

Approach

From west follow the directions on *page 9* for the north side of Ardnamurchan and, after clearing Sgeir Charrach, keep at least ½ mile off the east side of Rubha Aird Druimnich to avoid Bo Ruadh.

From north pass west of Sgeir an Eididh (11m high) off the east side of the bay and keep it in line with Rubh' Arisaig astern 353° to avoid a submerged rock, 1·3m, ¼ mile south-southeast of it.

Anchorage

Anchor in about 5m, south of Dubh Sgeir (1m high) towards the south end of the loch.

Caolas Ardtoe

A narrow inlet on the east side of Loch Ceann Traigh, ½ mile southeast of Sgeir an Eididh, leading to Kentra Bay which completely dries.

There appears to be reasonable anchorage in the narrows in 3m, sand, but the tide runs quite strongly through the channel, to and from Kentra Bay.

The plan, based on a 19th-century Admiralty survey, has been included in small-boat sailing directions since 1984.

Approach

A landmark for the entrance is a prominent sand dune above the bay four cables south of the entrance. Steer east-southeast towards Rubha Lingan at the north side of the entrance and keep ¼ cable from that side until the entrance narrows, to avoid drying rocks extending from the south side of the entrance.

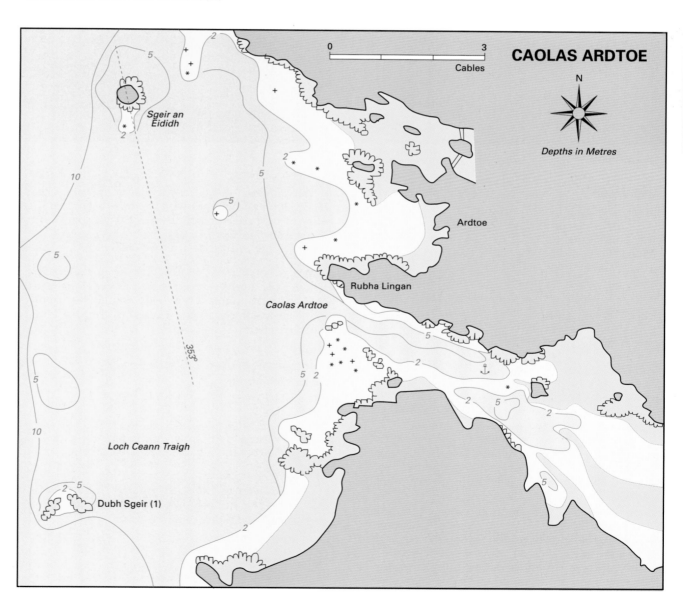

Caolas Ardtoe

Anchorage

Either one cable west-northwest of the islet which lies ½ mile east-southeast of Rubha Lingan, or ½ cable south of it.

Shoal-draught boats can take the ground on sand off the stone slip ¼ mile further southeast on the north side of the inlet (any yacht with a reasonably long keel could dry out alongside for repairs if necessary).

Loch Moidart

⊕ West of Eilean Raonuill 56°47'·2N 5°53'·5W

One of the most picturesque of all West Coast lochs with sandy beaches between rocky headlands and, further in, a ruined castle on a tidal islet with thickly wooded shores on either side.

It is however one of the most difficult of all lochs to enter with a labyrinth of islets and rocks, many of them submerged or drying, and the courses to be taken on transits of islets have to be quickly identified in turn.

A steep sea builds up in the entrance when the ebb is running against a westerly wind, which is particularly likely to trouble a small yacht when leaving the loch.

The entrance lies three miles south-southwest of the south point of the Sound of Arisaig and 2½ miles east of Rubha Aird Druimnich.

Eilean Shona on the north side of the entrance is 263m high and merges with the hills behind it; it is easy to mistake either the North Channel or Caolas Ardtoe for the main entrance to Loch Moidart.

Charts

There is no current detailed chart of Loch Moidart. Photocopies of the very old chart *531* (*see Appendix I*) will provide more detail than anything currently published, subject to the usual reservations about obsolete charts.

Tides

Constant –0048 Ullapool (–0508 Dover)

Height in metres

MHWS	MHWN	MTL	MLWN	MLW
4·8	3·5	2·6	1·6	0·5

During and after heavy rain the level of high water may be raised significantly with a significant stand at HW, and a consequent accelerated rise and fall.

Approach

From the west as for north side of Ardnamurchan (*see page 11*); Rubha Aird Druimnich bearing 263° astern will lead direct to the entrance.

From the north keep clear west of Howorth Rock which has a least depth of 1·9m, ¾ mile off the middle of the west side of Shona, unless you are satisfied that there is no swell and there is sufficient height of tide for your draught. The 20m contour is a safe guide here.

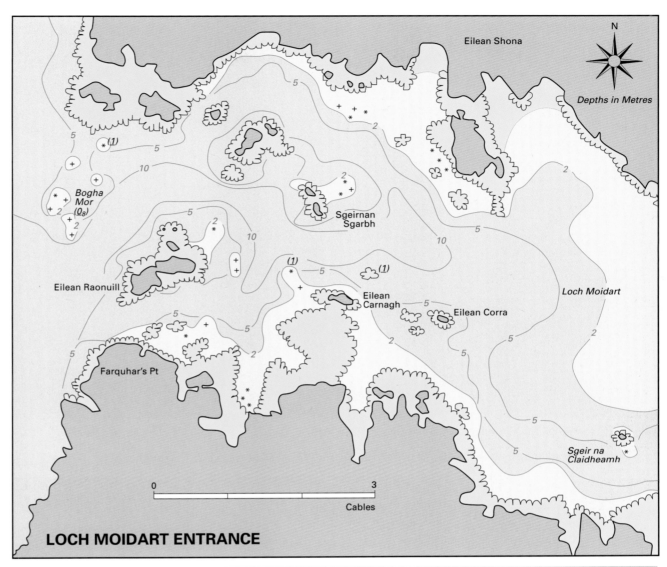

LOCH MOIDART ENTRANCE

Loch Moidart approach. Eilean Raonuill at the right is identified by a perch on its summit

Eilean Raonuill in the middle of the entrance, 11m high with a thin perch on its summit, must be positively identified.

Castle Tioram, two miles further east, hidden behind Eilean Raonuill bearing 094° leads south of rocks on the north side of the passage northwest of Eilean Raonuill.

Eilean Raonuill can be passed on either side but the north side is the most straightforward.

To pass north of Eilean Raonuill steer northeast to pass ¼ cable north of rocks above water on a drying reef on the north side of Eilean Raonuill.

When the east end of Eilean Raonuill is abeam head for Sgeir nan Sgarbh, a prominent rock above water 1¾ cables east-northeast of Eilean Raonuill, in line with the south point of Shona 097°, then pass ¼ cable south of Sgeir nan Sgarbh.

Eilean Corra, east-southeast of Eilean Raonuill, is conical in shape, rather like a limpet and Sgeir na Claidheamh (pronounced approximately as 'clay') stands to the southeast of it. When Sgeir na Claidheamh is open east of Eilean Corra, turn to pass east of Eilean Corra and ½ cable south of Sgeir na Claidheamh to avoid a detached drying rock.

Loch Moidart entrance. Eilean Raonuill stands to the right of the boat's wake, and Sgeir nan Sgarbh immediately above

Loch Moidart entrance from southeast. Eilean Raonuill is towards the top left and Eilean Corra towards the right

The passage south of Eilean Raonuill is narrower than that to the north, with more dangers.

Approach the centre of the passage heading 073° to avoid a drying reef off the southwest point of the island and drying rocks east of Farquhar's Point.

Identify Eilean Carnagh and Eilean Corra east-southeast and, when they are in line, steer for the south point of Sgeir nan Sgarbh and then proceed as described for the passage north of Eilean Raonuill.

Several temporary anchorages can be found here but more satisfactory ones lie further in.

To continue further up the loch, approach to within about a cable of Shona, although note that a reef which extends from Shona has been reported to extend further than expected.

Close west of Riska a shallow bar of sand crosses the loch, and underwater cables, apparently disused, cross the loch both east and west of Riska; their landing places are unmarked.

Anchorages

The most straightforward is ½ cable east of the jetty on Shona but this is quite exposed in southerly winds, particularly at HW.

Castle Tioram in Loch Moidart

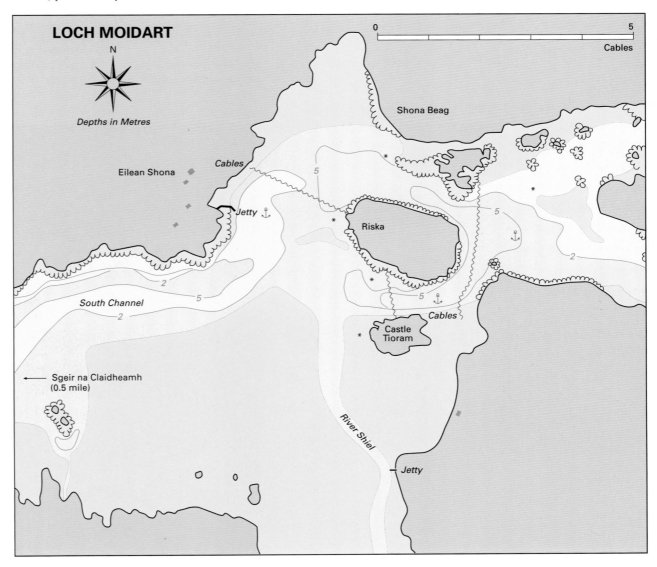

East of Riska, a cable northeast of a rock above water off the south point of the loch there.

South of Riska, off the east end of the castle island.

If approaching from the west note that the sand bar is shallower southwest of Riska than northwest, and there are drying rocks off the southwest side of Riska.

In all cases take great care to avoid the lines of cables. Each of these anchorages is subject to fairly strong tides.

Further east most of the loch dries, with a narrow channel following the south shore. It can be explored with a dinghy or shoal-draught boat with the aid of the old chart *531*.

Supplies

The nearest stores are at Acharacle, about four miles by the road south of the castle. Phone box ½ mile along the same road.

Castle Tioram is considered unsafe and has been fenced off; note that the spit joining the island to the mainland covers at HW.

Loch Moidart, north channel

56°48′N 5°52′W

The main difficulty here is to identify correctly the rocks at the entrance.

Pass between the two Sgeir dhu's (their suffixes mean 'east' and 'west' although they are north and south of each other) heading for an islet close to the south shore.

An alternative approach is from southwest, passing east of Sgeir dhu an Iar.

Bogha Stru, which dries 1·4m lies well south of the row of skerries on the north side of the channel, and another rock drying 2·3m lies about a cable northwest of it (*see photo*). If only one drying rock can be seen, it is likely to be the one which dries 2·3m, and care must be taken to avoid Bogha Stru.

Bo Tony, the detached submerged rock in mid-channel is only a hazard to a yacht of moderate draft at LWS – but it is a real hazard.

Thereafter keep in the middle of the channel, but closer to the south side as the bar is approached.

The bar has a depth of 1·8m and the tide runs strongly over it. Anchor as far up the inner basin as depth allows.

A drying bank prevents access to the main part of Loch Moidart except for dinghies and very shallow-draught boats at HW.

If there is any sea running, entering and particularly leaving, this anchorage could be a matter of some anxiety.

Moidart North Channel from northwest, about half tide

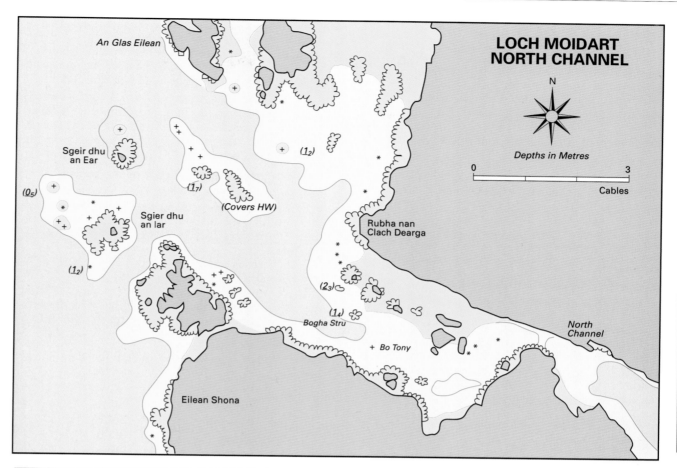

Loch Moidart North Channel. Bogha Stru stands to the left of the middle of the photo towards the far side of the channel, with the rock drying 2·3m further to the left

Sound of Arisaig

56°51′N 5°52′W

This is the main inlet on this part of the coast with an entrance two miles wide between Rubh' a' Phuill Bhig on its south side and a group of islets near the Arisaig Promontory on the north side. The south shore is clean outwith a cable from the shore, but there are many rocks above and below water up to a mile off the north side.

Tides

Constant −0048 Ullapool (−0508 Dover)

Height in metres

MHWS	MHWN	MTL	MLWN	MLWS
4·8	3·5	2·6	1·6	0·5

Streams within the Sound are generally weak.

Approach

Eilean an t-Snidhe, 10m high, lying one mile south of the Arisaig promontory must be identified.

Pass at least ½ mile south of that island to avoid various submerged rocks.

To pass north of this group keep the north end of Eigg, bearing 300°, just open of Eilean a' Ghaill, which lies off the Arisaig promontory, north of Eilean an t-Snidhe.

Gulnare Rock, at a depth of 2·7m, lies a mile east of Eilean an t-Snidhe, and Astly Rock, least depth 0·9m, lies 1½ cables south of the Borrodale Islands.

Both of these are avoided by keeping the north end of Muck open south of Eilean an t-Snidhe 265°.

Priest Rock off the mouth of Loch Ailort is cleared on its west side by keeping the summit of Sidhean Mor, the highest hill on the north side of the sound, open west of the end of Ardnish Peninsula on the north side of Loch Ailort 031°.

Anchorages in the outer part of the sound

Glenuig Bay, 56°50′N 5°49′W, 1¼ miles east of Rubh' a' Phuill Bhig, provides some shelter but the rocks in the mouth of the bay all cover and do not provide much protection from any sea from the west or northwest.

Two perches mark rocks on either side of a passage south of the west rock.

There are several moorings in the bay, and the jetty is used by local boats. Anchor between the jetty and the west rock, clear of the approach to the jetty.

Supplies

Hotel, shop, *Calor Gas* one mile up the glen. Phone box.

Glenuig Bay from west

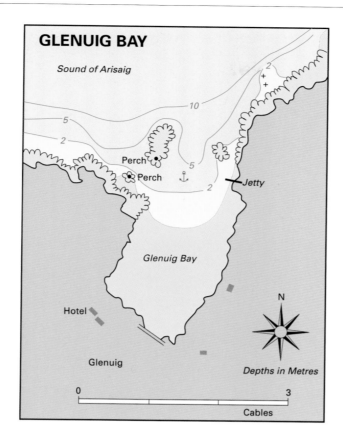

GLENUIG BAY

Sound of Arisaig

Perch

Perch

Jetty

Glenuig Bay

Hotel

Glenuig

Depths in Metres

0

3

Cables

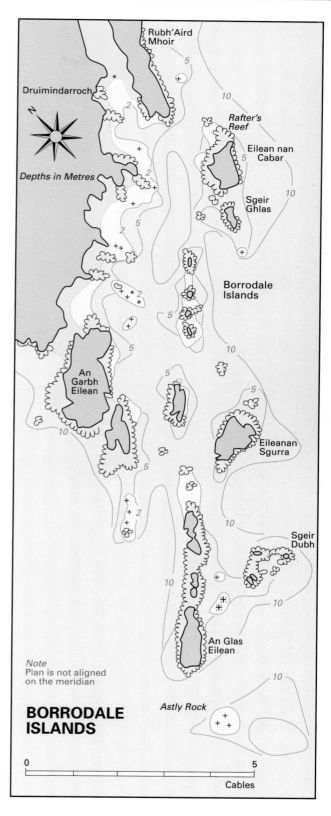

Rubh'Aird Mhoir

Druimindarroch

Depths in Metres

Rafter's Reef

Eilean nan Cabar

Sgeir Ghlas

Borrodale Islands

An Garbh Eilean

Eileanan Sgurra

Sgeir Dubh

An Glas Eilean

Note
Plan is not aligned
on the meridian

BORRODALE ISLANDS

Astly Rock

0

5

Cables

On the north side of the sound several inlets provide occasional anchorages, in particular Port nam Murrach (*see photo on page 27*), Port a' Bhathaich, and Port Doire na Drise. The approach to each of them is straightforward using chart *2207*.

Borrodale Islands

56°53'N 5°49'W

A string of islands on the north side of the sound providing some, although not complete, shelter.

The best anchorage is at Druimindarroch at the north end of the group, easily identified by a large conspicuous house.

Eilean nan Cabar is identified by six pine trees on its summit, and the white sandy beaches on the southeast side of Rudh' Aird Mhor show up clearly.

Rafter's Reef, which dries, extends almost halfway across the passage north of Eilean nan Cabar (*Cabar* is Gaelic for 'rafter').

The anchorage is best approached by the north of Eilean nan Cabar as a perch which formerly marked a drying rock southwest of Eilean nan Cabar is missing.

Give the northwest end of Eilean nan Cabar a good berth and keep closer to the mainland than to the island to avoid Rafter's Reef.

Anchorage

Anchor in the bay north of Eilean nan Cabar clear of moorings and clear of a submerged rock off the east point of the bay.

Borrodale Islands from north, about high water. Druimindarroch at bottom left and Eilean a' Cabar at left

Loch nan Uamh

56°53'N 5°46'W

At the head of the loch (56°53'·5N 5°44'W) there is a deep anchorage on the east side of Eilean Gobhlach or, in southerly winds, on the north side of Ard nan Buth.

The pool east of Eilean a' Phuill may be entered by keeping towards the east side to avoid a drying rock in the middle of the entrance.

Loch Ailort

⊕ Two cables south of Sgeir Ghlas 56°50'·6N 5°47'·2W

The outer part of the loch is fairly open, but Eilean nan Gobhar (Goat Island) and Eilean a' Chaolais at the mouth of the loch provide some shelter and the outer anchorages are quite easy to approach.

There are quite heavy overfalls around the islands when the ebb tide runs against a strong westerly wind.

Winds between south and east produce heavy squalls from the mountains.

Navigational buoys may be installed by fish farm operators, but these have no official status and cannot be relied upon.

Navigation of the middle part of Loch Ailort is as difficult as any in this chapter, with the usual crop of drying rocks, and islets which are difficult to identify.

Beyond the narrows, 2½ miles from the entrance, mountains close in on either side.

Dangers and approach

Priest Rock, four cables west-northwest of Goat Island, dries 1·4m and there is no good clearing mark for it. In the passage north of Goat Island, a submerged rock lies ½ cable north of the island.

The most straightforward entrance is by the south of Goat Island. If passaing south of Goat Island keep at least a cable south of the island to avoid drying rocks south and southeast of it.

The narrow passage north of Eilean a' Chaolais may be used in quiet weather, but note drying rocks up to a cable northeast of the island.

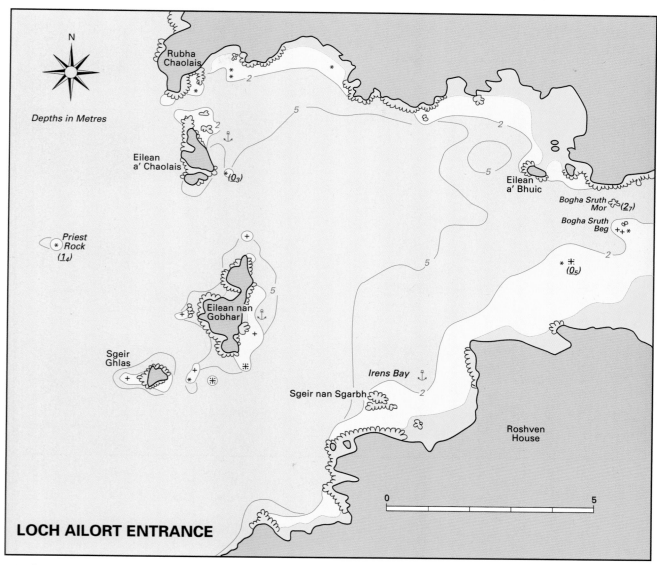

LOCH AILORT ENTRANCE

Depths in Metres

Anchorages

Goat Island (Eilean nan Gobhar) provides the best shelter in westerly winds, off a stony beach on its east side.

This is traditionally regarded as the most suitable anchorage in the Sound of Arisaig to run for in heavy weather, although it would be unlikely to be comfortable.

The wind funnels through a gap in the middle of the island.

A submerged rock lies ½ cable off the south end of the pebble beach.

Eilean a' Chaolais, close east of the island.

A drying rock southeast of the island is cleared by keeping Sgeir Ghlas touching the west side of Goat Island.

In quiet weather anchor anywhere in the bight northeast of the island, but note drying rocks up to a cable northeast of the island.

Irens Bay off Roshven House on the south shore. Suitable in light offshore winds; anchor well offshore, between Sgeir na Sgairbh and the northeast point of the bay, as it is very shoal.

Loch Ailort, middle part

56°51'N 5°44'W

About ¾ mile east of Goat Island the loch narrows to ⅓ mile wide. The south side of the channel is shoal and drying, with rocks drying 0·5m about mid-channel. Eilean a' Bhuic lies west of the north point of the entrance to this channel.

Near the north shore, Bogha Sruth Mor and Bogha Sruth Beg cover about half-tide. Bo Sruth Mor to the north is slightly higher than Bo Sruth Beg.

In the next mile the channel twists between shoals and drying rocks.

Approach before half-flood so that the Bogha Sruths are visible, and pass between them. If both are covered, there is enough depth to pass north of Bogha Sruth Mor within ¼ cable of the shore.

After passing these rocks head for the southern half of Eilean nan Trom; then bring the east end of Eilean na Gualainn in line with the west end of Eilean nam Bairneach 140°, to pass between a drying rock west of Eilean nan Trom and a drying bank a cable further west.

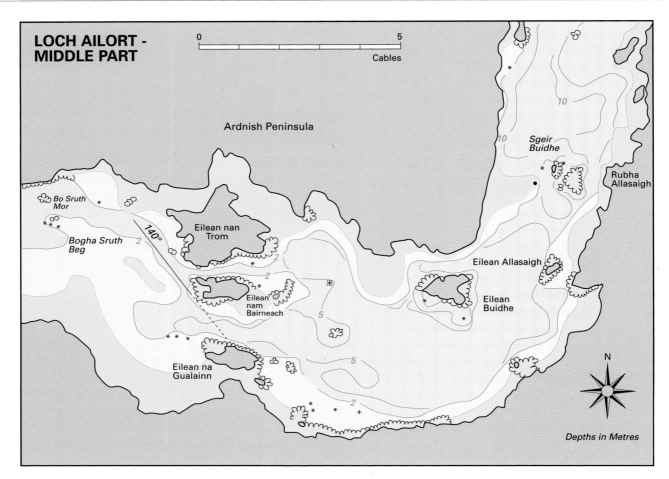

**LOCH AILORT -
MIDDLE PART**

0   5
Cables

Ardnish Peninsula

Bo Sruth
Mor

Bogha Sruth
Beg

Eilean nan
Trom

Eilean
nam
Bairneach

Eilean na
Gualainn

Sgeir
Buidhe

Rubha
Allasaigh

Eilean Allasaigh

Eilean
Buidhe

N

Depths in Metres

Loch Ailort entrance *Jean Lawrence*

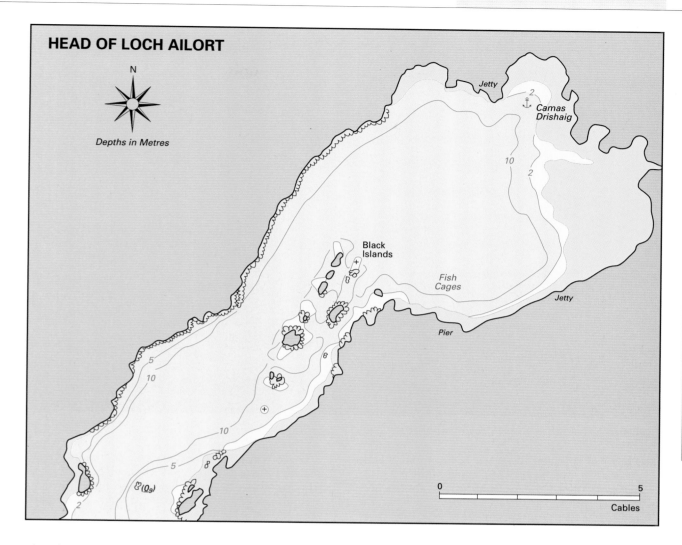

HEAD OF LOCH AILORT

N

Depths in Metres

Camas
Drishaig
Jetty

Black
Islands

Fish
Cages

Jetty

Pier

0   5
Cables

The channel between Eilean nan Trom and Eilean nam Bairneach may be taken; a line to clear the drying reef a cable east of Eilean nam Bairneach is the north end of Goat Island touching the south point of Eilean nan Trom 272°.

Alternatively pass west of Eilean nam Bairneach, keeping ½ cable off that island, and follow round to pass midway between Eilean nam Bairneach and Eilean na Gualainn.

After the east end of Eilean na Gualainn has been passed, its north point in line with the most northerly point of the south shore, 278°, leads south of Bogha Druim a' Loch. South of that line is a designated area for permanent moorings, and a designated anchorage lies immediately to the east, off the south shore south of Eilean Buidhe.

There are no other regular anchorages here, nor at the head of the loch, but if your taste for rock-dodging hasn't been exhausted, the following will guide you through the upper part of the loch.

Head of Loch Ailort

56°52'N 5°41'W

Keep at least a cable south of Eilean Buidhe to avoid a drying rock, pass about ½ cable northwest of Eilean Allasaigh and steer towards Rudha Allasaigh, three cables further north-northeast.

Pass about ¼ cable off the point of Rudha Allasaigh to avoid a large area of rocks which covers at HW, ½ cable from the shore.

The spit on the west side, west of these rocks, has a boulder at its outer end which covers above half-tide.

If the boulder is visible, an alternative course is to pass about 30m east of it, heading north-northwest.

About four cables further north a rock in the middle of the loch dries about 0·9m; it lies midway between two tidal islets, one on either shore. The rock appears to be in line with two white marks on the northwest shore.

A mile further northeast the Black Islands (Eilean Dubh) lie on the southeast side of the loch. A survey of 1860 shows moderate depths among them, with a bottom of sand as well as some rock.

Note the submerged rock one cable south of the most southerly above-water rock, as well as a drying rock ¼ cable off the east shore.

Loch Ailort narrows from Roshven *Jean Lawrence*

The head of the loch is a deep basin about ¾ mile across with an extensive fish-farming industry.

The east side of the basin dries for about three cables and the most suitable anchorage is at the mouth of Camas Drishaig on the northeast side of the basin.

Loch nan Ceall (Arisaig Harbour)

⊕ On leading line two cables south of Luinga Mhor 56°53'·7N 5°56'W

One of the most intimidating entrances of any anchorage on the West Coast, although much easier now that the perches are regularly maintained.

As the Admiralty *West Coast of Scotland Pilot* put it in 1934:

'This tortuous channel, being full of rocks, is dangerous to enter, and as the islets in the vicinity are low and inconspicuous they are of no assistance in fixing the position of a vessel.'

The perches, which have been restored by Arisaig Marine, make the entrance channel possible for a stranger – once he has found the entrance.

Rubh' Arisaig is identified by a white paint mark, visible from at least 10 miles.

Additional perches have been established and the existing perches renewed. These consist of posts about 15cm in diameter without topmarks, all red to port and green to starboard. A pair of lateral buoys mark the heads of sandbanks on either side of the channel where it opens up into the inner basin.

Charts

A photocopy of chart *2817*, published in 1858 (1:10,700) provides the greatest detail, subject to the usual reservations about using obsolete charts (*see Appendix I*).

Note also that present-day perches do not correspond to those on the old chart.

Names of features are taken from that chart.

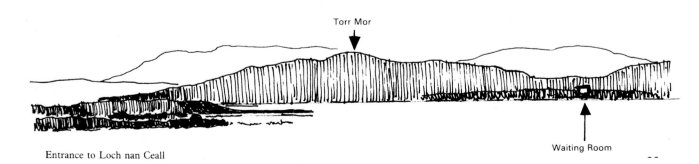

Entrance to Loch nan Ceall

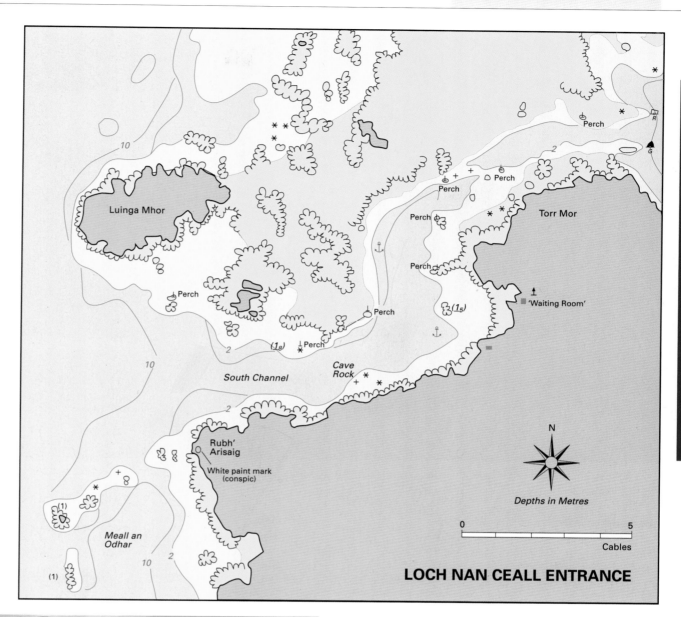

LOCH NAN CEALL ENTRANCE

(Map labels: Luinga Mhor, Torr Mor, Perch (multiple), 'Waiting Room', South Channel, Cave Rock, Rubh' Arisaig, White paint mark (conspic), Meall an Odhar, Depths in Metres, N, 0 ... 5 Cables)

Rudh' Arisaig. Port nam Murrach lower right

Tides

Tidal streams run strongly in the entrance channel, particularly for 1½ hours either side of LW when the banks on either side of the channel are uncovered and the flow is concentrated within it.

Constant –0040 Ullapool (–0500 Dover).

Height in metres

MHWS	MHWN	MTL	MLWN	MLWS
5·0	3·8	2·9	2·1	0·7

Identification

The north point of Muck astern (not Eilean nan Each, which lies northwest of Muck) bearing 256° in line with the southeast point of Eilean Chathastail, southeast of Eigg, leads to the north side of entrance.

In poor visibility note that Luinga Mhor is low and flat.

Rubh' Arisaig stands up rather more than Luinga Mhor and has a patch of white paint on its end, which shows up well from the west.

Arisaig entrance channel with the white paint mark on Rubh' Arisaig clearly showing in the foreground

Dangers and marks in the approach

Meallan Odhar (Maol Rocks) stand up to ½ mile west-southwest of Rubh' Arisaig. The outermost rocks are 1m high.

On the north side of the entrance rocks drying up to 3·7m extend more than a cable south of the line between Luinga Mhor and the Fraoch Eilean, the islet three cables southeast of it.

A rock which just dries, almost two cables south of Luinga Mhor is marked by a red perch.

A rock which dries 1·8m two cables southeast of Fraoch Eilean is marked by a red perch. Little of the perch shows at HWS.

Unmarked drying rocks lie between these two perches, but a bit outwith the line joining them, so that particular care must be taken not to confuse them.

A third red perch lies two cables east-northeast of the second. The rock which it marks covers at HW springs and extends about 20m south of the perch.

Cave Rock, lying about a cable off the south shore and nearly two cables south of the third perch, dries at LW.

The Waiting Room (so called because it used to provide shelter for passengers waiting for steamers) is an inconspicuous grey cottage standing on the east shore, ½ mile east of the third perch.

Approach

From south keep at least a cable west of Meallan Odhar and north of Rubh' Arisaig, and pass one cable south of the first two perches.

The Waiting Room in line with a prominent dip in the hills immediately behind it bearing 080° leads clear between the dangers in the entrance.

From north it is essential to identify Luinga Mhor and pass southwest of it; yachts have in the past mistaken the passage and attempted to enter north of the island, with disastrous results.

Steer southeast towards the north side of Rubh' Arisaig until the red perches and the Waiting Room are identified, and pass a cable south of the perches

Anchorages

Temporary anchorage can be found either ¼ mile west of the Waiting Room or, in better shelter, north-northeast of the third perch, on the west side of the channel.

The entrance channel

The perches may be difficult to pick out at HW when little of them is showing, or at LW when they are hidden among the labyrinth of rocks. Owing to the twists of the channel each perch seems to appear in a surprising place in relation to the previous one. Make quite sure that each perch is the one you think

Arisaig entrance channel showing how difficult it would be to pick out the channel without beacons

Arisaig Channel

it is. Although much more securely established than in the past, marks may be missing, especially at the beginning of the season.

After the third red perch, the channel turns north, with two green perches marking reefs on the east side of the channel, and a red perch to the north of them. Steer about 010° with the red perch fine on the starboard bow, and give the second green perch a respectful berth as Bogha Sruth Mor which it marks extends ½ cable northwest of it.

Take care to avoid confusing a third green perch, Bogha Sruth Beg for Bogha Sruth Mor, and Bogha Ruag red perch for the fourth red perch.

Having passed Bogha Sruth Mor steer 060° to pass south of the red perch and north of the third green perch, Bogha Sruth Beg. A rocky ridge lies east to west between the red perch and Bogha Sruth Beg, but there is at least 1.5m over it.

Continue on a heading of 060° towards a fifth red perch, Bogha Ruag to avoid a sand bank which encroaches on the south side of the channel; pass south of Bogha Ruag and steer 090° to pass between a pair of lateral buoys marking the east end of sandbanks on either side of the channel.

Note that fishing floats may well be encountered here.

Continue heading 090° towards a group of single-storey cottages on the east shore to pass between a pair of perches, and give Rubha Daraich on the north shore a fair berth as the rocky foreshore dries off for half a cable. Do not stray from the fairway as the basin is littered with unmarked drying rocks.

Keep a careful check astern at this point to make sure you are not being set off course, especially if entering against the ebb.

On leaving Arisaig, steer west for the first pair of perches, and then the pair of buoys at the entrance to the channel. Keep towards the first two red perches in the channel, and when clear past the second green perch turn south, in line with a road on the shore ahead. Leave a green perch to port and a red to starboard and when past this turn to head 260° to pass a cable south of two red perches.

Arisaig Harbour

56°54'·5N 5°51'W

Arisaig village lies at the east side of a basin, about 1½ miles from Bogha Ruag, the last perch in the entrance channel.

South of the village stands a group of low cottages and, south of them again, several detached houses among trees.

From a point ½ cable south of Bogha Ruag steer for the three low cottages and keep them bearing 090°.

Anchorage

Anchor clear of moorings off the pier in the northeast corner of the basin, and clear of the approach to the pier which is used regularly by the passenger boat *Sheerwater*.

Alternatively pick up a mooring temporarily and immediately make contact with Arisaig Marine to check that it is free.

Arisaig North Channel from west – not for the faint-hearted

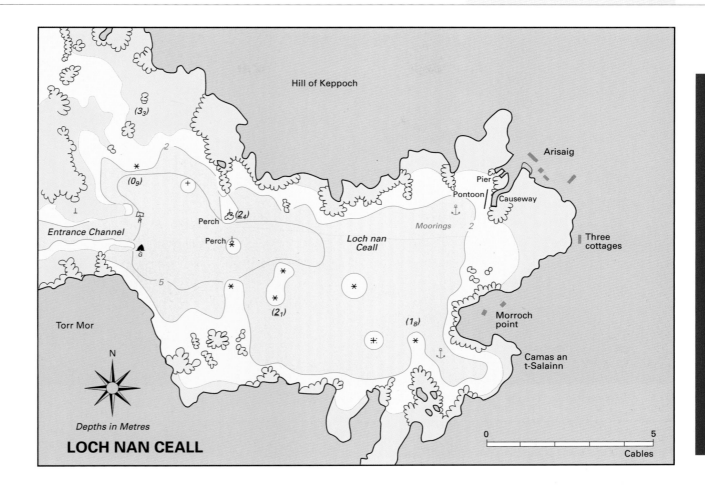

Hill of Keppoch

(3₃)

2

*

(0₉)

+

⊥

Entrance Channel

Perch

Perch

Loch nan Ceall

Moorings

2

Pier

Pontoon

Causeway

Arisaig

Three cottages

Morroch point

Camas an t-Salainn

Torr Mor

5

(2₁)

(1₈)

N

Depths in Metres

LOCH NAN CEALL

0   5

Cables

The inlet at the pier dries at LW springs; yachts may go alongside on a rising tide if access is not needed for the *Sheerwater*. Keep the south face of the pier well open to avoid reefs at the entrance.

Yachts may also go alongside a pontoon at the new causeway south of the old pier (much more conspicuous, in fact, than the pier itself) to take on water or stores but check that access will not be needed for the *Sheerwater*.

Trailed boats may be launched from a slip at the head of the inlet if the slipway is not occupied (ask first).

Camas an t-Salainn in the southeast corner of the basin is occupied by private moorings.

Services and supplies

Moorings, repairs, diesel, *Calor Gas*, water at pier and at pontoon. Slipway with cradle on rails. Shop, hotel, restaurant.

Communications

Post office, phone box, train and bus to Mallaig and Glasgow. Arisaig Marine ☎ 01689 450224.

North Channel

North of the skerries in the entrance lies the North Channel, of which the current Admiralty *Pilot* drily observes, 'it is seldom used, even by vessels with local knowledge'. It would be impossible to provide directions; use the old chart in combination with the photo if you must try it.

Passage notes

North of Loch nan Ceall, drying rocks extend more than a mile from the shore; in poor visibility keep outwith the 15m contour or set a compass course to avoid the risk of following the coastline in among the rocks.

Morar River

56°58′N 5°50′W

A river estuary five miles north of the entrance to Loch nan Ceall with a winding channel, in which the depth is mostly less than half a metre, between inviting banks of white sand, which feature regularly in Tourist Board brochures.

The entrance has a bar, on most of which there is no more than 0·2m and the position of the deepest part varies.

Morar Estuary from west. The spit outside the bar can be seen, lower right

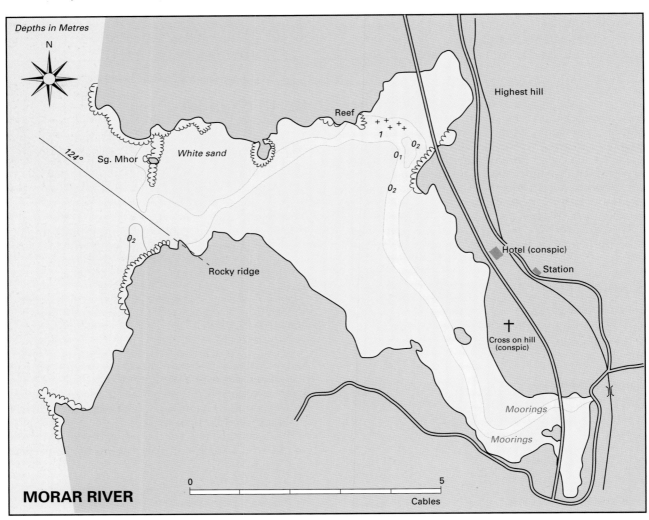

The slightest swell would make the entrance hazardous even to a shoal-draught boat except perhaps during the last quarter of the flood.

Several yachts are kept on moorings at the head of the estuary, but there must be many occasions when the sea on the bar makes it impossible to go out.

A keelboat might find a place to lie afloat at the most northerly point of the channel at neaps, the river is only suitable for twin-keel and shoal-draught yachts.

The photo should be studied closely as there is no detailed survey. A sand spit usually extends northwest from the south point of the entrance and a succesful approach is only likely to be made from that direction. Pass one cable west of Sgeir Mhor steering about 124° towards a ridge of rock about 20m high, east of the the south point of the entrance and then follow the channel by eye in the clear water.

Supplies

Shop, hotel, garage, Post Office, phone box.

Mallaig

⊕ ½ cable north of light buoy north of Sgeir Dhearg
57°00'·8N 5°49'·5W

This busy fishing harbour and ferry terminal lies at the south point of the entrance to Loch Nevis, 7½ miles north of Loch nan Ceall. Its main attraction is the wide range of services available, but yachts have to take their chance among working boats. There

may be space to anchor in the southeast corner of the harbour. The attitude to yachts is more positive than has been found in the past.

A new basin has been built but is subject to scend and is not much used.

Glaschoille, on the north side of Loch Nevis, four miles from Mallaig, may be found more peaceful in northerly winds.

Charts

2208 (1:50,000); plan (1:7,500) on chart *2534*

Tides

The constant is –0050 Ullapool (–0500 Dover)

Height in metres

MHWS	MHWN	MTL	MLWN	MLWS
5·0	3·8	2·9	2·1	0·7

Approach

If possible, call up the harbourmaster before entering for advice on where to berth.

From south and west Eilean na h-Acairseid and large industrial buildings on Rubha na h-Acairseid, east-northeast of the island, help to identify the entrance in poor visibility.

The passage between the new breakwater and Sgeir Dhearg is not recommended.

A G con light buoy has been laid northeast of Sgeir Dearg.

Traffic signals three vertical red lights at the head of the Steamer Pier indicate that a large vessel is

Mallaig. Look out for ferries and fishing boats

I. ARDNAMURCHAN TO MALLAIG

entering or leaving the harbour, and small craft should keep clear of the entrance.

Lights

At night, the lights may be difficult to identify against the lights of the town.

Sgeir Dhearg Fl(2)WG.8s6m5M
Buoy G con Q.G
Steamer Pier extension Iso.WRG.4s6m9-6M, with a separate light Fl.G.3s14m6M

Anchorage

Anchor in the southeast corner of the harbour or as directed by the harbourmaster. There are many moorings and the bottom is foul. Moorings may be available from the harbourmaster or the boatyard.

Supplies and services

Boatyard, engineer, diesel, petrol, *Calor Gas*, water at pier.

Chandler and Admiralty chart agent. Shops, including chemist and butcher (within Spar supermarket), bank, hotels. For water and diesel call the harbourmaster before berthing. A self-service fuel dispenser in the new harbour is operated by obtaining a PIN from Johnston Bros, or delivery by tanker may be arranged elsewhere in the harbour.

Showers at RNMDSF.

A cash machine located inside the CalMac waiting rooms at the ferrry terminal can be accessed during normal port opening hours.

Communications

Train and bus to Glasgow, ferry to Skye, Post Office, telephone.
Harbourmaster VHF Ch 09
℡ 01687 462154 (outside working hours ℡ 462411).
Boatyard (Henderson) ℡ 01687 462304.
Chandler and chart agent (Johnston Bros)
℡ 01687 462215.

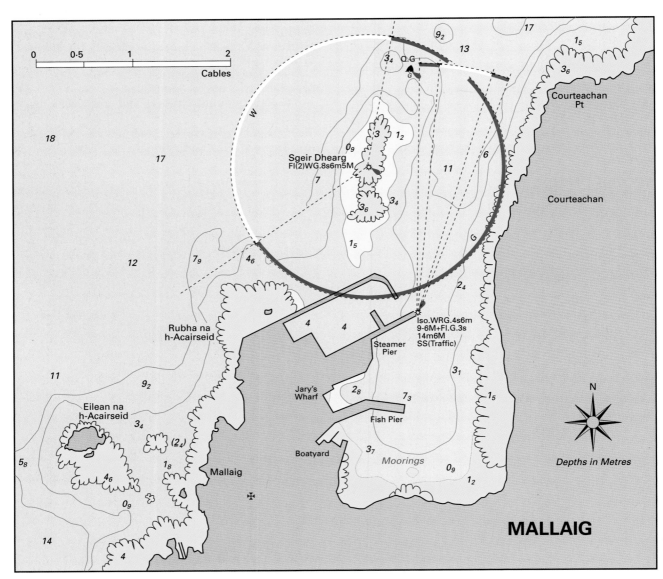

II. The Small Isles

The group of four islands between Ardnamurchan and Skye, each inhabited by a small community and each of very different character.

Only Canna, the most northwesterly of the Small Isles, has a good sheltered anchorage and it makes an ideal staging post on the way to the Outer Hebrides.

Charts

The only charts showing the Small Isles in any detail are *2207* and *2208* at 1:50,000. Even these don't include the whole of Canna; chart *1795* does so, but only at 1:100,000. *OS Explorer map 397* neatly covers all the Small Isles at 1:25,000 and *OS Landranger 39* at 1:50,000.

Tides

On the west side of Eigg the constant averages −0048 Ullapool (−0508 Dover).

Height in metres

MHWS	MHWN	MTL	MLWN	MLWS
4·7	3·5	2·6	1·6	0·5

Among the Small Isles the flood stream runs generally northwestwards and northwards, and both flood and ebb reach a rate of 4kns in places, particularly east of Eigg, between Muck and Eigg, and around the rocks between Canna and Hyskeir.

Heavy overfalls occur wherever there are relatively shallow banks.

Steep seas are reflected off the west point of Rum in strong westerly winds.

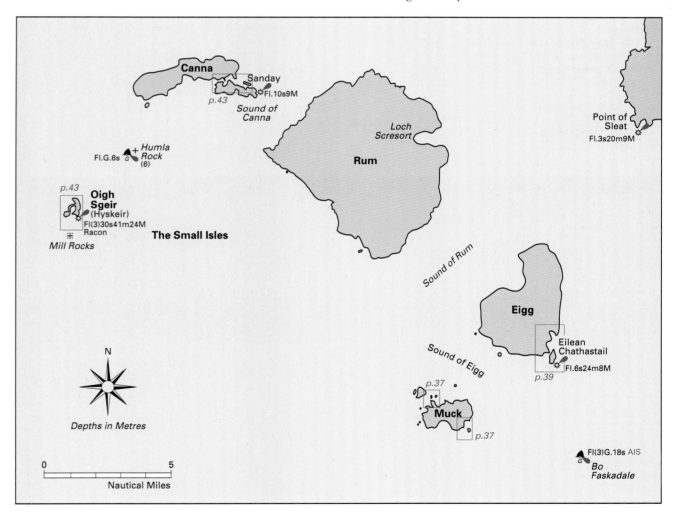

Among the Small Isles the streams turn approximately as follows:

The north-going stream begins +0600 Ullapool (+0140 Dover)

The south-going stream begins HW Ullapool (−0420 Dover).

Dangers

Many drying rocks extend up to ¼ mile off the shores of the Small Isles so that the chart must be carefully studied before approaching the shore.

Banks and rocks east and southeast of Eigg and Muck are described in the previous chapter.

In the passage between Muck and Eigg, six cables north of Muck, Godag is a group of rocks of which the most southerly is above water, with drying and submerged rocks up to three cables further north.

Southwest of Canna there are several rocks between Canna and Hyskeir (Oigh Sgeir) and there is some doubt as to the completeness of the survey here.

Marks

The best identification is the shape of the islands themselves. Rum is high and mountainous; Eigg has the long ridge of the Sgurr lying on an east-west axis at its south end which from the east looks like a rock pinnacle.

Good use can be made of transits of the edges of any two islands, and this is particularly valuable as there are several magnetic anomalies in the area.

Lights

Ardnamurchan lighthouse Fl.20s55m24M
Eigg (SE point of Eilean Chathastail) Fl.6s24m8M
Canna (E end of Sanday) Fl.10s32m9M
Hyskeir (Oigh Sgeir) Fl(3)30s41m24M
Bo Faskadale buoy 6M NE of Ardnamurchan Fl(3)G.18s

ISLE OF MUCK

Muck is an attractive island to visit and, short of a failure of the weather forecasts, one anchorage or the other should provide adequate shelter. Port Mor is well marked and lit for the new ferry terminal, although space for yachts to anchor is reduced.

The island has been run successfully as an agricultural estate by the McEwen family for very many years.

Port Mor

⊕ On leading line 318° southeast of Sgeir Dubh
56°49'·2N 6°12'·7W

At the southeast side of the island, Port Mor is the main harbour, but the rocks at the entrance do not completely protect it from any sea from south.

Dubh Sgeir, an above-water rock, lies in the middle of the entrance, with drying reefs joining it to the west point of the inlet and extending ½ cable all round.

Bogha Ruadha, a detached drying reef, lies about a cable to the east of Dubh Sgeir, south of a drying reef extending ¼ mile south of the east point of the inlet.

A shoal patch with a depth of less than 2m lies in the passage between these two rocks.

Light beacons are being established on either side of the fairway, with a Port Entry Light on the shore, and a ferry terminal has been built on the east side of the harbour.

Muck. Port Mor while the new ferry terminal was being constructed

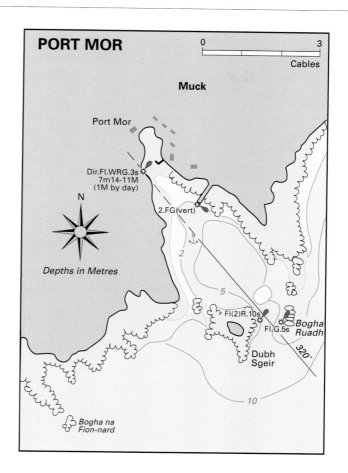

PORT MOR

Muck

Port Mor

Dir.Fl.WRG.3s
7m14-11M
(1M by day)

N

2.FG(vert)

Depths in Metres

Fl(2)R.10s

Fl.G.5s

Bogha Ruadh

Dubh Sgeir

320°

10

Bogha na Fion-nard

0 — 3

Cables

Approach

From south steer northeast to pass southeast of Muck until it is clear open southwest of Eigg; identify the settlement by reference to the wind generators at the east end of the island, bring the generators fine on the starboard bow heading 318° and pass between the light beacons.

From east or northeast, keep the east shore of Muck open of the west shore of Eigg, bearing 360° astern, until the approach is identified, to clear Bogha Ruadh, and steer 318° as above.

Lights

Port Entry Light DirFl.WRG.3s9m14/11M 322°
Port-hand bn Fl(2)R.10s4m3M
Starboard-hand bn Fl.G.5s4m3M
Jetty head 2F.G(vert)7m2M

Anchorage

On the west side of the inlet, clear of the ferry terminal and fairway.

Small shoal-draught boats may find space to dry out in complete shelter behind the L-shaped stone jetty at the head of the inlet.

A new jetty, which also dries, has been built on the northeast side of the inlet.

Supplies

No supplies. Phone box near the old pier.

Gallanach (Bagh a' Ghallanaich)

⊕ ¼ mile north of Bohaund 56°51'·1N 6°15'·5W

The entrance to this bay on the north side of Muck is obstructed by drying reefs, but these only offer limited protection from seas from the north.

Tides

Tides run at 4kns at springs in the Sound of Eigg, between Eigg and Muck, as well as on the west side of Muck, but less strongly across the mouth of the bay itself.

Dangers and marks

Horse Island (Eilean nan Each) is attached to the northwest point of Muck by drying reefs.

Godag, a detached rock six cables north of Muck, about a mile east of Horse Island, has drying and submerged rocks ¼ mile north of it.

Drying reefs extend several cables northwest from the east point of the bay.

Bohaund, a detached reef which dries 1·2m, lies in the middle of the entrance.

Approach

From east pass south of Godag, and head for the north end of Horse Island.

The gap between Lamb Island (Eilean Ard nan Uan) and Lamb Point, immediately south of it, appears as a square notch in the skyline. When this closes, head for the south end of Lamb Island, keeping the gap well closed, to clear the reef on the east side of Gallanach Bay.

A line which leads between Bohaund and the reef to the east, consists of a barn with a curved roof

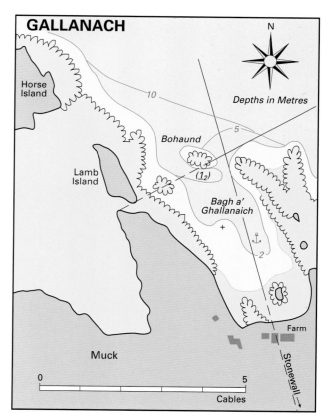

GALLANACH

N

Horse Island

10

Depths in Metres

5

Bohaund

Lamb Island

(1₂)

Bagh a' Ghallanaich

2

Muck

Farm

Stonewall

0 — 5

Cables

(now painted dark green) at the west side of the farm under the highest point of a stone wall on the left shoulder of the hill beyond; a newer barn (which is not the one you want) has been built close west of the first one.

About two cables south of Bohaund lies a rock awash. Anchor north or northwest of the tidal islet towards the head of the bay.

ISLE OF EIGG

⊕ ¼ mile southwest of Eilean Chathastail 56°52′N 6°08′·5W

Eigg is the most easterly of the Small Isles and has a substantial population, most of whom live at the northwest side of the island.

The main anchorage (56°53′N 6°08′W) lies at the southeast side, in the channel between Eigg and Eilean Chathastail, but the shelter is not very good. A drying berth is provided alongside the north side of the ferry terminal.

Tides

Constant averages +0132 Ullapool (−0508 Dover)
Height in metres

MHWS	MHWN	MTL	MLWN	MLWS
4·7	3·5	2·6	1·6	0·5

The tide runs strongly through the anchorage, the flood running northwards, turning south two hours before HW.

Off the east side of Eigg streams run at 4kns at springs, causing a heavy sea with wind against tide, and making approach from the east difficult.

Gallanach Bay, Muck, from north-northwest. Bohaund is just visible in the middle of the mouth of the bay

Dangers and marks

Eilean Chathastail is 35m high, grass-covered, with a white light beacon on its southeast side.

Drying rocks extend a cable south and southwest of Eilean Chathastail. A clearing mark is Eilean Chathastail open of the eastern extremity of Eigg.

A Port Entry Light (DirFl.WRG.3s9m14–11M) stands on the east end of the ferry terminal, with the centre line bearing 245°.

Light columns stand on the southeast side of Flod Sgeir (Fl.G.10s4m3M), and on the north side of Garbh Sgeir (Fl.R.10s4m3M).

Approach

From south keep two cables off the southwest point of Eilean Chathastail to avoid the drying reefs there. Rubha na Crannaig, the east point of Eigg, open west of the north point of Eilean Chathastail 028° leads clear of these reefs (*see photo*).

From south by the east side of Eilean Chathastail, keep clear of the southeast shore of the island, as a reef extends some way offshore, and clear of Garbh Sgeir. In winds between north and east, anchor in the south bay southwest of Galmisdale Point.

From east identify the perch on Flod Sgeir and pass ¼ cable southeast of it heading southwest for Sgeir nam Bagh, then south towards Galmisdale Point.

Anchorages

South of Galmisdale Point clear of reefs which dry one cable from northwest side, and also clear of the strong tide in the narrows.

North end of Eilean Chathastail. There is not usually space to anchor near the jetty owing to the moorings, and there is a risk of fouling ground tackle.

A berth drying 1m has been incorporated in the north side of the causeway at the ferry terminal. The approach channel to this berth from the east is marked by single unlit red and green perches.

Poll nam Partan, ½ mile north of Eilean Chathastail, has a depth of 2·5m at the deepest part, but the approach from south just dries.

Eigg. The leading line to clear reefs on the west side of Eilean Chathastail is the island open of Eigg

Enter the pool above half tide between Flod Sgeir and Eigg, keeping the east side of Sgeir nam Bagh in line with the west side of Eilean Chathastail.

Experienced navigators, especially using Antares charts, can approach this pool from east-southeast. The rock north-northeast of Flod Sgeir is awash at chart datum, so that this approach should be easy above half tide.

Anchor on sand clear of rock or weed, easily visible in the clear water, wherever depth and swinging room can be found.

All of these anchorages are only safe in moderate weather.

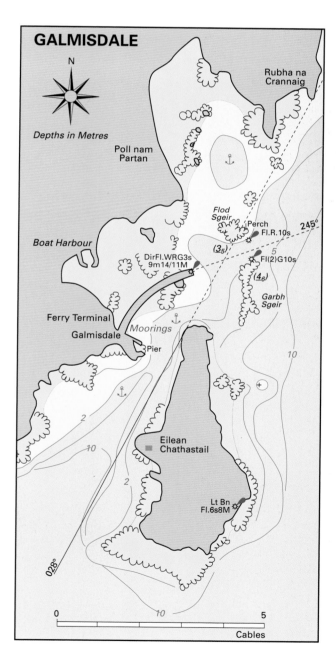

Eigg. Poll nam Partan from southeast. Garbh Sgeir at lower left, Flod Sgeir is about the middle of the photo. The photo was taken before the ferry terminal was built

Eigg, Galmisdale from northwest near HW. The drying yacht berth is about the centre of the photo *Patrick Roach*

Supplies and services

Diesel, water, *Calor Gas*, restaurant, coffee shop at jetty; showers, small shop, telephone.
Ferries to Mallaig and Arisaig.
Isle of Eigg Heritage Trust ① 01687 482486

Laig Bay on the northwest side of Eigg provides occasional anchorage in offshore winds. The bay is notable for its 'singing sands' in certain conditions.

Isle of Rum

The largest of the Small Isles, Rum is spectacularly mountainous. Access is much more liberal than hitherto and the following is an extract from a letter from the Reserve Officer:

'Rum is a National Nature Reserve managed by the government agency Scottish Natural Heritage (SNH). The island is of national and international importance for its plants, wildlife and geology.

Whilst important research does take place on the island, visitors are still made very welcome and we actively encourage people to come and enjoy the magnificent scenery and wildlife Rum has to offer.

Occasionally people are asked to avoid certain areas for conservation or safety reasons (for example, in late spring/early summer certain lochans have breeding populations of the rare red-throated diver, which are particularly sensitive to human disturbance) but these restrictions are kept to an absolute minimum.'

Rum has excellent walks offering outstanding views of Skye and the Hebrides. Tours of Kinloch Castle are run throughout the summer season. The island also has a small shop where a good range of supplies can be purchased.

The Castle Bistro offers reasonably-priced evening meals, but you are asked to book a day in advance.

Dog owners are asked to keep their dogs on a lead at all times and not to take them beyond the deer fence surrounding Kinloch. Dogs may not be kept ashore overnight.

Some further restrictions apply to a deer enclosure at Kilmory, and anyone planning a more extensive visit, including climbing and hill-walking, should contact the Reserve Office, Isle of Rum, PH43 4RR, ① 01687 462026.

Kinloch Castle, built in 1903, has been used as an hotel but is currently closed, apart from the tours mentioned above.

Dangers

Off the north point of Rum several drying rocks lie up to ¼ mile from the land; these are avoided by keeping outwith the 15m contour.

At the west point of Rum drying reefs extend one cable from the shore, and any sea from the west is reflected and becomes particularly steep and confused.

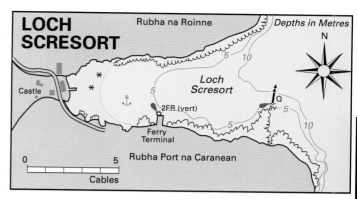

Loch Scresort

⊕ Mid entrance to Loch Scresort 57°01'N 6°24'W

An inlet more than a mile long on the east side of Rum, shoaling very gradually towards the head, subject to violent squalls in strong westerly winds, and swell with easterly winds.

Drying reefs extending nearly ¼ mile from the south shore at the entrance are marked by a north cardinal light buoy, and there are drying rocks close inshore on the north side.

The bottom is sand with patches of weed.

A roll-on ferry terminal has been built on the south shore of Loch Scresort (2F.R.vert).

Approach

Keep well off the south shore on entering, and anchor off the concrete slip on the south side of the loch, or northeast of the stone pier further in.

Supplies

Basic stores at shop. Phone box and Post Office.

ISLE OF CANNA

Canna is the most westerly of the Small Isles with a well sheltered natural harbour, often used by yachts on passage to the Outer Hebrides, as well as by fishing boats. Its climate is better than its neighbours, having no mountains to the west, and it has white sandy beaches.

Canna was presented to the National Trust for Scotland by John Lorne Campbell, its owner for many years.

Canna Harbour

⊕ Northeast of Sgeir a' Phuirt 57°03'·5N 6°34'W

Dangers and marks

Rocks off the north coast of Rum referred to above must be avoided by keeping at least half a mile off shore.

The north side of Canna is clean beyond a cable from the shore.

Between the south side of Canna and Hyskeir there are several rocks for which chart *1795* must be consulted (*see also Hyskeir, on page 43*).

Canna Harbour (photographed before the new ferry slip). The buildings which serve as leading marks can be seen upper left

Canna is notorious for anchors picking up weed

Canna Harbour *Patrick Roach*

The east point of Sanday on the south side of Canna Harbour is marked by a small but conspicuous white light beacon.

Sgeir a' Phuirt, an extensive reef between the light beacon and the harbour entrance, dries 4·6m, two cables north of Sanday.

Inside the harbour on the southwest side of Rubha Carrinnis, the north point of the entrance, is a concrete pier and ferry terminal. The ferry slip is built over the drying rock shown which extends beyond the side of the slipway.

West of the pier lies a drying rock which will be incorporated in the ferry terminal, with a shoal spit southwest of it.

The harbour shoals gradually towards the northwest shore, with a clean sandy bottom.

Compass Hill at the northeast point of Canna causes abnormal magnetic variation to the east of Canna.

Approach

Identify the farm towards the west end of the harbour and keep it in line with the south side of Rubha Carrinnis to lead north of Sgeir a' Phuirt.

Keep to the south half of the entrance to avoid the rock west of the pier. This rock can be avoided by keeping a conspicuous cottage on the hillside open southwest of the southwest end of a pair of cottages on the shore.

Lights

Sanday light beacon Fl.10s32m9M is obscured between 061° and 152°.
Leading lights on Sanday bearing 233° (front Q, rear Iso.4s)
Sgeir a'Phuirt R can light buoy Fl.R.2s
Rubha Carrinis Fl.G.3s
Lights at the pier, 2F.G(vert).

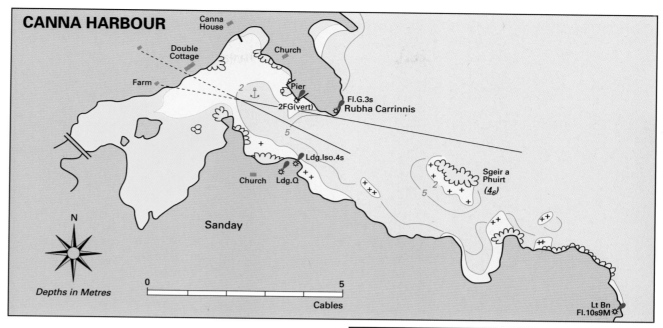

CANNA HARBOUR

Canna House
Double Cottage
Church
Farm
Pier
2FG(vert)
Fl.G.3s
Rubha Carrinnis
Ldg.Iso.4s
Church Ldg.Q
Sgeir a Phuirt (4₆)
Sanday
N
Depths in Metres
0 5
Cables
Lt Bn Fl.10s9M

Anchorage

Anchor wherever there is enough depth; a good guide is to bring a prominent white stone cross in the churchyard on the northeast side of the harbour under the summit of Compass Hill.

Fishing boats used to congregate in Canna Harbour during the hours of darkness, but there are now few of them. Nevertheless, show a good anchor light and, if you use a tripping line, secure it inboard.

There is enough weed on the bottom for new arrivals to provide plenty of entertainment for those already securely anchored.

Supplies

No supplies. Phone box and Post Office at the pair of cottages on the northwest side of the harbour.

The south side of Canna should not be approached without both charts and OS *Explorer map 397*.

Canna Boat Harbour The bay between the west end of Sanday and the south side of Canna provides a temporary anchorage in very quiet weather.

There are many rocks in the approach and Sgeirean Dubha, 2m high, in the middle of the entrance, is the key to the approach.

A rock which just dries, four cables southwest of the entrance, is cleared by keeping Sgeirean Dubha in line with the summit of Compass Hill bearing 051°.

Pass between Sgeirean Dubha and the rock northwest of it which covers at HW.

Tarbert Bay (57°03′N 6°32′W) lies a mile west of Sanday, southeast of a dip in the skyline of Canna.

Identify Haslam, an islet three cables off Canna, rather closer to the west side of the bay than to Sanday.

Keep at least ¼ mile off Haslam and approach the bay, keeping closer to its west side than to Haslam.

Anchor towards the northeast side of the bay, clear of rocks.

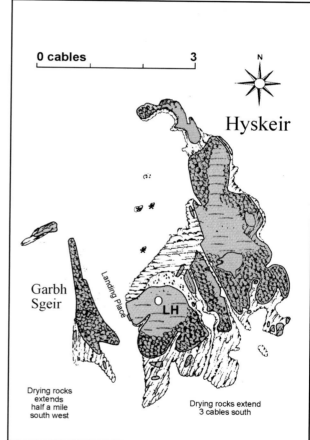

0 cables 3
N
Hyskeir
Garbh Sgeir
Landing Place
LH
Drying rocks extends half a mile south west
Drying rocks extend 3 cables south

Hyskeir (Oigh Sgeir)

56°58′N 6°41′W

A group of low islets five miles southwest of Canna with a white lighthouse 39m high.

It is only rarely visited by yachts and it is not recommended as there is almost no shelter.

Hyskeir from south-southeast. Drying rocks lie in the bay northwest of the lighthouse

Thomasina at Hyskeir on a very rare quiet day. Note that the landing place at any Northern Lighthouse Board property is no longer maintained, and NLB can accept no responsibility for damage or injury associated with any unauthorised landing

Dangers and marks

Humla Rock, 5m high, lying between Hyskeir and Canna, has a green conical light buoy (Fl.G.6s) on its southwest side.

Submerged rocks and shoals lie around Humla, and between that rock and Canna.

The usual passage from Ardnamurchan to the Minch lies between Hyskeir and the Humla buoy.

Mill Rocks, 2¼ miles southwest of Hyskeir, have depths of less than 2m. For a further three miles southwest seas break in strong winds owing to the uneven bottom.

The north point of Eigg just open of the south point of Rum 085° leads 1½ miles south of Mill Rocks.

A white lighthouse 39m in height stands on Hyskeir. Radar beacon (Racon).

Approach and anchorage

To anchor at Hyskeir the following course has been followed: pass one cable west of the north end of Hyskeir and steer 170° to keep open the narrow channel between Hyskeir and Garbh Sgeir on its west side, to avoid a drying rock in the bay northwest of the lighthouse.

Although this course has been taken successfully in the past, it should certainly not be assumed that there are no other rocks around.

The landing place is on the east side of the channel between Hyskeir and Garbh Sgeir, and there are three mooring rings on Garbh Sgeir opposite the landing place. The bottom is sand, with a depth of about 3m.

Many rocks lie off the south end of the channel, so that an approach from that direction should not be attempted.

III. West coast of Skye

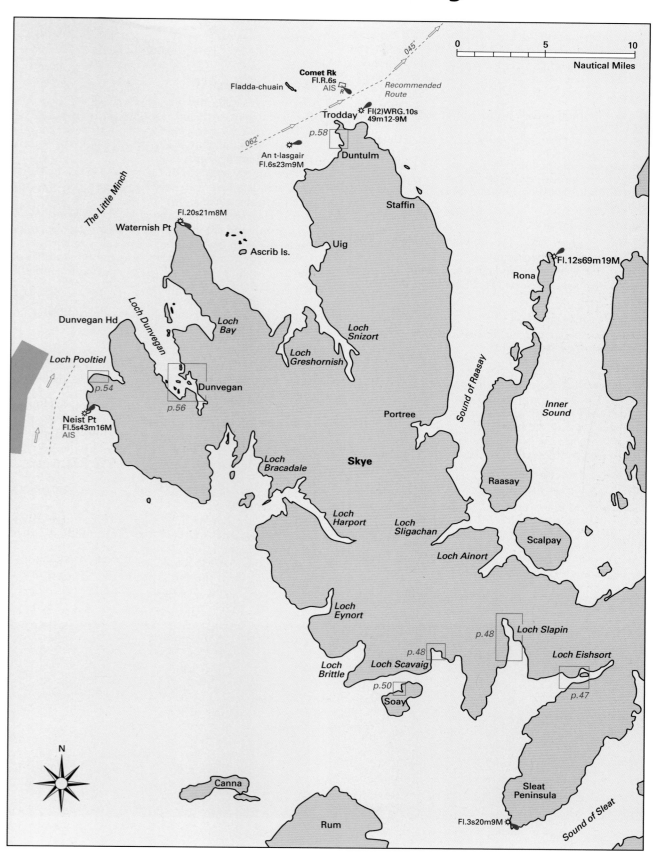

Comet Rk
Fl.R.6s
Fladda-chuain
AIS

Recommended
Route

045°

0   5   10
Nautical Miles

Trodday
☼ Fl(2)WRG.10s
49m12-9M

062°

p.58

An t-lasgair
Fl.6s23m9M

Duntulm

The Little Minch

Staffin

Fl.20s21m8M
Waternish Pt

Ascrib Is.

Uig

Fl.12s69m19M

Rona

Dunvegan Hd

Loch Dunvegan

Loch
Bay

Loch
Snizort

Loch Pooltiel

Loch
Greshornish

Sound of Raasay

Inner
Sound

p.54

Dunvegan

p.56

Portree

☼ Neist Pt
Fl.5s43m16M
AIS

Loch
Bracadale

Skye

Raasay

Scalpay

Loch
Harport

Loch
Sligachan

0

Loch Ainort

Loch
Eynort

Loch Slapin

p.48

Loch Eishsort

p.48

Loch Scavaig

p.47

Loch
Brittle

p.50

Soay

N

Canna

Sleat
Peninsula

Fl.3s20m9M

Rum

Sound of Sleat

Point of Sleat to Soay

Charts

2208 (1:50,000)
OS map Landranger 32
From Loch Eishort to Loch Brittle and all between
see *OS Explorer maps 412* for Sleat Peninsula and
Loch Eishort, and *411* for Loch Slapin to Loch
Eynort.

Tides

The north-going stream begins about +0535 Ullapool
(+0115 Dover)
The south-going stream begins about –0025 Ullapool
(–0445 Dover)
On the west side of Point of Sleat there is probably an
eddy with the north-going stream, and overfalls occur
west and southwest of the point with both flood and
ebb tides.

Dangers and marks

Point of Sleat is low and rocky with a 7m white light
beacon at its southwest tip.

Rocks, above water and drying, extend 1¾ cables
west of the point to Sgeir Dhubh which is 0·3m high.

Lights

Point of Sleat Fl.3s20m9M
Sanday (southeast of Canna) Fl.10s32m9M
Mallaig (*see Chapter I*)

Shelter

Moderate shelter may be found in Loch Slapin, Loch
Eishort (difficult approach), and Soay Harbour
(which has a tidal sill). Canna (*see Chapter II*)
provides some of the best shelter in the area. If heavy
westerly weather is expected, consider Sound of Sleat
(*see Chapter IV*), Mallaig or Arisaig (Chapter I).

Occasional anchorages

Tarskavaig, 57°07′N 6°00′W, and Ob Gauscavaig
(Tokavaig), a mile northwest of Tarskavaig, provide
occasional anchorages in settled weather.

Supplies

Nearest (limited) at Rum; otherwise Mallaig, Arisaig
(*Chapter I*), or Loch Harport below.

Loch Eishort

57°10′N 5°55′W

Tides

Constant –0040 Ullapool (–0500 Dover)
Height in metres

MHWS	MHWN	MTL	MLWN	MLWS
4·8	3·7	2·8	2·1	0·7

Dangers and marks

Drying reefs extend more than a cable southwest of
Rubha Suishnish, the north point of the entrance.

Two miles further east the loch narrows abruptly
with islets and drying rocks up to ½ mile off Rubha
Dubh Ard at the south side.

Sgeir an t-Sruith, about four cables north of Dubh
Ard, stands above water with drying reefs extending
from it to the north shore.

A drying reef extends about ¼ cable south of Sgeir
an t-Sruith and drying reefs also lie up to two cables
north of Dubh Ard, leaving a passage ¼ mile wide.

Many rocks which cover lie in the next 1½ miles
but one, which lies north of Sgeir Gormul on the
chart, rarely if ever covers.

There appears to be a discrepancy on chart *2208*:
Sgeir Gormul itself covers at half tide and is not, as
shown on the chart, above water.

Directions

At a state of tide when Sgeir Gormul will be visible,
pass one cable south of Sgeir an t-Sruith, then steer
northeast to bring Sgeir Gormul clear of the
southeast point of Eilean Heaste onto a line to clear
scattered rocks off the south shore. Steer to pass
south of Sgeir Gormul and north of the rock drying
4·8m, ¼ mile east. Pass south of another rock at a
similar height in mid-channel south of Eilean Heaste
to avoid rocks on the north side. Not less than a
cable east of Eilean Heaste turn north and anchor off
Heaste village.

Pass either side of the group of rocks three cables
further east and south of the most southerly rock
south of Heaste Island.

Continue east for ¼ mile before turning north and
anchor north of the fish cages in the bay east of the
island.

Tarskavaig from east

Ob Gauscavaig from west

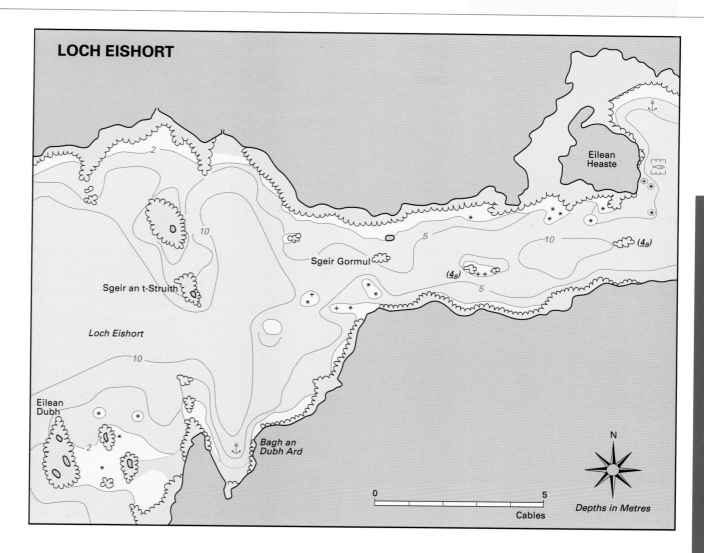

LOCH EISHORT

Eilean
Heaste

Sgeir Gormul

(4_8)

Sgeir an t-Sruith

(4_8)

Loch Eishort

Eilean
Dubh

Bagh an
Dubh Ard

N

0 — 5

Cables

Depths in Metres

Loch Eishort from south of Sgeir an t-Sruith

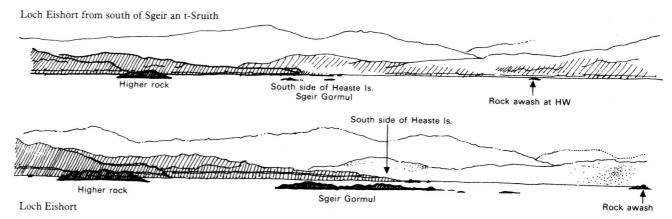

Higher rock

South side of Heaste Is.
Sgeir Gormul

Rock awash at HW

South side of Heaste Is.

Higher rock

Sgeir Gormul

Rock awash

Loch Eishort

Anchorage

Bagh an Dubh Ard, on the south side of the narrows, is an occasional anchorage; when approaching from the west keep closer to Sgeir an t-Sruith than to Dubh Ard to avoid reefs off Dubh Ard; the bottom shelves steeply.

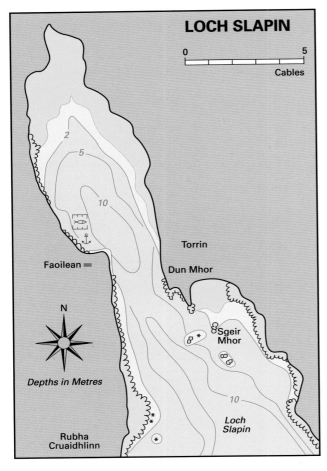

LOCH SLAPIN

Loch Slapin

57°12'N 6°01'W

Tides

Constant −0040 Ullapool (−0500 Dover)

Height in metres

MHWS	MHWN	MTL	MLWN	MLWS
4·8	3·7	2·8	2·1	0·7

Dangers and marks

Fierce gusts can be expected from the hills at the head of the loch and blowing out of the entrance.

Bogha Ailean lies ¼ mile off the west shore two miles north-northeast of Strathaird Point at a depth of 1·8m; the southeast point of Rum open of Strathaird Point 212° clears this rock.

Drying reefs extend more than a cable southwest of Rubha Suishnish, the east point of the entrance.

Sharp blocks drying and just submerged lie off Rubha Cruaidhlinn.

Rocks drying and awash lie south and west of Sgeir Mhor on the east side of the loch.

Anchorage

The head of the loch dries off for ½ mile and the best anchorage lies on the west side close to the south shore of Bagh nam Faoilean which is steep-to, or north of the fish cages there.

Services

Post Office, telephone at Torrin. Water tap at Faoilean.

Loch Scavaig

⊕ In fairway east of Eilean Reamhar 57°11'·4N 6°09'·5W

This anchorage can claim to be the most spectacular on the West Coast, surrounded by the jagged peaks of the Cuillin Hills; however the squalls there tend to be equally spectacular.

The 4th edition of the Admiralty *Pilot*, dated 1894 described the Loch in the following words:

'Gairsbheinn, the southern mountain of the south-western ridge, overlooks loch Scathvaig and Soa island. It assumes a remarkable and picturesque appearance; the summit, 2,902 feet high, is like the edge of a knife and so narrow as scarcely to leave room for the erection of a pile of stones. The south-eastern face forms an arc of a circle to the water's edge, nearly as perfect as could be drawn, with three distinct cliffs separated by steep sloping ledges, round which the sheep walk and are frequently blown over by the rushing gusts of wind, and killed. During a heavy fall of rain, the southern and south-western sides of

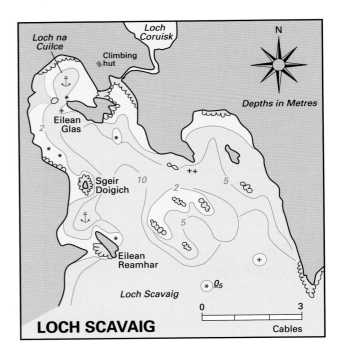

LOCH SCAVAIG

Loch Slapin

Dun Mor

Loch Scavaig, Loch na Cuilce in the foreground and the anchorage at Eilean Reamhar beyond

this mountain which, though smooth, are exceedingly steep, present a most singular appearance; the dark heavy cloud round its summit is strongly contrasted by a thousand rills and torrents which pour down its sides and form a perfect network, whilst the two swollen burns at its foot, fall over the cliff in broad and roaring waterfalls. Few more singular and awful sights can be witnessed than the view from the anchorage under Soa, when, during the pauses of a heavy SW gale, the wind and rain suddenly cease, the lower atmosphere clears and discloses the scene described.

Loch Scavaig approach. Eilean Glas stands in front of the white cottage, and the approach is round the west end of the island

In northerly winds, which come on very unexpectedly, the gusts descend the steep sides of Gairsbheinn in sudden and most violent squalls, driving a cloud of foam, like a water spout, before them with a roar like thunder and almost before it has time to drive a vessel at anchor to the extent of her chain, the gust has passed, and for a few moments it is quite calm.'

Tides

Constant –0040 Ullapool (–0500 Dover)

Height in metres

MHWS	MHWN	MTL	MLWN	MLWS
4·8	3·7	2·8	2·1	0·7

Dangers

Drying rocks lie in the middle of the loch leaving a passage 1¼ cables wide east of Eilean Reamhar which lies on the west side of the loch; drying rocks also lie ¼ cable northeast of Eilean Reamhar.

Sgeir Doigich 1½ cables north of Eilean Reamhar occasionally covers, and drying rocks lie off the west shore a cable further northwest.

Loch na Cuilce

A shallow pool at the head of Loch Scavaig behind Eilean Glas; the entrance to the pool by the west end of Eilean Glas is ¾ cable wide, but a broad drying rock lies 55m west of the island. Another small drying rock lies about 10m north of the west end of Eilean Glas, and a submerged rock lies close southwest of the island.

Approach

Identify Eilean Reamhar and pass ½ cable east of it as well as Sgeir Doigich.

Pass 20m west of Eilean Glas; if the rock west of Eilean Glas is visible it may be passed on its west side although there is less depth there.

It is particularly important to leave swinging room clear of other boats already anchored, as squalls may drive a boat in any direction round her anchor. There are some mooring rings ashore, but their use may be more of a hindrance than help. Bottom thick mud.

An alternative anchorage lies west of the north end of Eilean Reamhar, 13m mud and thick weed.

Landing steps at the northeast side of Loch na Cuilce are used by tourist boats from Elgol, and dinghies must be left clear of the steps.

Soay Sound

57°10′N 6°14′W

Tides

The tidal stream sets permanently to westward. Confused sea is set up at the west end of the sound with south or southwest winds.

Constant –0040 Ullapool (–0500 Dover)

Height in metres

MHWS	MHWN	MTL	MLWN	MLWS
4·8	3·7	2·8	2·1	0·7

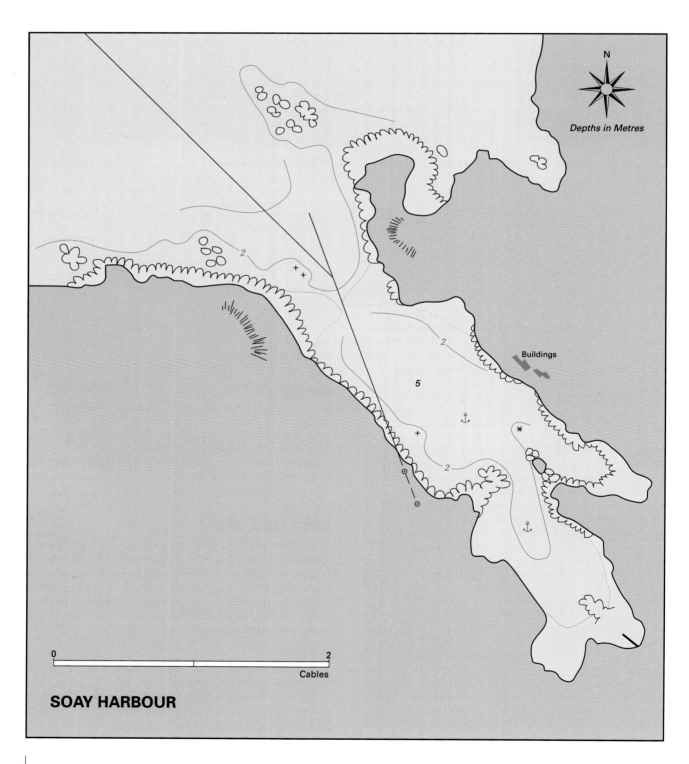

SOAY HARBOUR

Soay Harbour showing the channel at the bar, and the drying rock south of the jetty

Soay Harbour

The inlet on the north side of Soay is less than a cable wide.

A shingle bar across the entrance dries 0·6m in the channel, which lies slightly northeast of the middle of the entrance.

Reefs extend ½ cable from the south shore and more than a cable northwest from the northeast point of the entrance.

Approach

Not before half flood, heading southeast towards the buildings and jetty on the northeast shore to avoid drying reefs on the east side; two white poles on the southwest shore in line lead through the deepest part of the channel at the bar. The poles, especially the rear pole, may be difficult to identify among the trees.

Dangers and marks

A rock which dries 0·6m lies less than ½ cable south of the jetty and a drying reef extends towards this rock from the southwest shore, but a narrow passage past the head of the reef leads to an inner pool.

Three moorings for fishing boats are laid in the harbour.

Other anchorages

An Dubh Chamas ¾ mile east of Soay Harbour is well sheltered from southerly winds but may be obstructed by a fish farm.

Camas nan Gall, on the south side of Soay, has poor holding on shingle.

Southwest Coast of Skye from Soay to Neist Point

⊕ One mile WSW of Neist Point 57°25′N 6°49′·5W

The shore of this part of Skye consists of cliffs rising to 285m with occasional inlets, of which only Loch Bracadale and Loch Harport offer any shelter.

A Traffic Separation Scheme exists off Neist Point, with related recommended tracks at the northeast end of the Little Minch.

Charts

1795 (1:100,000) (Loch Eynort is on chart *2208*)
OS *maps Landranger 23, 32. OS Explorer map 410*

Tides

Tidal streams between Soay and Loch Bracadale run at up to 1kn
The northwest-going stream begins +0535 Ullapool (+0115 Dover)
The southeast-going stream begins –0025 Ullapool (–0445 Dover)
Off Neist Point the northwest-going stream begins –0405 Ullapool (+0400 Dover)
The southeast-going stream begins +0220 Ullapool (–0200 Dover)
From +0535 to –0405 Ullapool (+0115 to –0400 Dover) the south-going stream meets a northwest-going stream and is deflected to the west. Thus, effectively, the stream is running northwest or west for nine hours out of 12.

Dangers and marks

A magnetic anomaly, which is strongest near the northeast point of Canna, affects all of the area between Loch Brittle and Idrigill Point.

An Dubh Sgeir, 5m high, 1½ miles from the shore and 3¼ miles west of Idrigill Point at the west side of Loch Bracadale, is the outermost of a line of rocks known collectively as the Mibow Rocks (Mi-bogha).

A passage ¼ mile wide lies between Mi-bogha Beag and Mi-bogha Mor.

Macleod's Maidens are a prominent group of rock stacks close to the shore southwest of Idrigill Point.

To pass between Mibow Rocks keep Macleod's Maidens bearing 112°.

Lights

Neist Point Fl.5s43m16M
Sanday (southeast of Canna) Fl.10s32m9M
Oigh Sgeir (Hyskeir) Fl(3)30s41m24M
Ardtreck Point light beacon, Loch Harport Fl.6s18m9M

At night

Keep Neist Point bearing more than 330° to clear An Dubh Sgeir.

Shelter

Loch Harport or Canna Harbour.

Minor anchorages

Ru an Dunain, 57°19′·4N 6°18′·5W. An interesting visit on a quiet day to visit the remains of the 'Viking Canal' which probably dates from the 16th century. Anchor on the east side of Sgeir Mhor, avoiding drying rocks lying about ½ cable south-southeast and

III. WEST COAST OF SKYE

Ru an Dunain with the 'Viking Canal'. Drying rocks lie near the shore on the right, outside the margins of the photo

a cable east-southeast of the Dun standing on a cliff at the east side of the inlet.

Loch Brittle 57°11'N 6°19'W. A very occasional anchorage, only if there is no swell; shop at camp site.

Loch Eynort, 57°14'N 6°22'W, occasional anchorage, if no sea from west. Subject to severe squalls from north.

An Dubh Sgeir, 5m high, off the southeast point has a clear passage inshore.

Stac a Mheadais, 24m high, stands close to the shore about one mile northwest of the entrance.

Fish traps extend south from the north point of the entrance.

It is reported that the reef on the north side of the entrance in approximate position 57°13'·8N 6°24'·2W may extend underwater further than is apparent.

Some shelter beyond the bend, off the northwest shore but the holding here has been found to be poor.

Good shelter and holding have been found in a gale from east and northeast close to the wooded shore on the east side at the corner.

Loch Harport

⊕ ½ mile west of Ru na Clach 57°18'·6N 6°29'·8W

A branch of Loch Bracadale, described below, although Loch Harport is more conveniently treated as a separate loch.

Tidal streams are insignificant, and the loch is free from hidden dangers.

Light

Ardtreck Point light beacon Fl.6s18m9M

Anchorages

Oronsay, west of Ardtreck, gives some shelter on the east side of the drying reef which joins the island to Skye.

A drying reef extends ½ cable southeast from the northeast point of the island.

The best landing place is reported to be in the SW bay on the southeast side of Ullinish Point.

Meals and showers at Ullinish hotel; advance booking is requested.

Loch Beg, northeast of the entrance, is a satisfactory anchorage only if there is no sea from the south. The bottom is soft and the holding has been found to be poor.

Several inshore fishing boats lie on moorings, and the end of a concrete slip on the west side is marked by a prominent perch.

Restaurant and Post Office up hill at the main road. Water from spring at stone basin near head of slip.

Gesto Bay, the next bay to the east, is good in offshore winds.

Port na Long, on the south side of the loch, opposite Loch Beg, provides better shelter in southerly winds.

Many inshore fishing boats lie on moorings, and the west side is occupied by fish cages. Anchor between the moorings and the fish cages. A jetty lies at the east side of the entrance, consisting of a

Loch Harport entrance, with Ardtreck light beacon on the right and Port na Long beyond

Loch Beag, Loch Harport, with the perch marking the end of the slip at the right. Rubha na Clach at upper right

Carbost, Loch Harport. Visitors' moorings lie off the trees east of the drying foreshore. A yellow buoy with a topmark marks an outfall pipe running over the foreshore northeast of the distillery

sloping deck on broadly-spaced piles; there is depth to go alongside at all states of the tide but it is not suitable to remain there.

The bottom of an apparently inviting area for anchoring consists of rock and kelp and may be busy with fishing and fish farm workboats.

Post Office, telephone, hotel, all ½ mile along road. Showers at 'The Bothy' bunkhouse, also cycle hire. *Calor Gas* at hotel.

Carbost on the south shore, 1½ miles from the head of the loch.

A shoal area extends out from the distillery burn, and there is a broader area with moderate depth beyond the shoal, below a war memorial, but the head of the loch dries off for nearly a mile.

Anchor near the southwest shore between the pier and the distillery.

Visitors moorings are laid in 5m east-southeast of the distillery.

The pier has a depth of about 2m alongside and is sometimes used by fishing boats; a yacht would need fender boards at the pier.

Supplies

Shop at Carbost, Post Office, Youth Hostel about one mile, hotel (meals), telephone at hotel. Water from tap outside public toilet. Tours of distillery.

Loch Bracadale

57°20′N 6°32′W

Tides

Constant –0050 Ullapool (–0510 Dover)
Heights in metres

MHWS	MHWN	MTL	MLWN	MLWS
5·1	3·8	2·9	2·1	0·8

Dangers and marks

Rubha nan Clach, the southeast point of the entrance, is a cliff 129m high.

Wiay, in the middle of the entrance is 60m high, flat-topped with cliffs all round.

Idrigill Point, the west side of the entrance, is identified by Macleod's Maidens, three rock stacks standing close southwest of it.

The outer part of the loch is free from hidden dangers and, although it has several branches, there is little shelter.

Anchorages

Oronsay The bay on its northwest side is clean but very restricted.

Tarner Island gives some shelter on its northeast side.

Loch Caroy, north of Wiay, provides little shelter.

Tarner Island, ¾ mile north of Wiay, may be passed on either side but, if on the east side, keep closer to Tarner than to Skye as drying rocks lie in the middle and to the east side of the passage.

Sgeir a' Chuain, 2m high, ¾ mile further north has drying reefs up to a cable round it, but can be passed on either side.

About ¼ mile north of Sgeir a' Chuain, drying reefs extend two cables from Crossinish Point on the west shore.

Anchor near the jetty on the east side, ½ mile from the head of the loch.

Loch Vatten is entered by the west side of Harlosh Island, 1½ miles northwest of Wiay.

Harlosh Skerry dries two cables west of Harlosh Point.

Poll Roag at the head of Loch Vatten can only be entered near HW by shallow-draught boats, but is traditionally a winter mooring for fishing boats. Holding is poor with weed and patches of soft mud.

Loch Bharcasaig, an inlet on the northwest side of Loch Vatten, with a forestry plantation at its head, is the best anchorage in Loch Bracadale other than Loch Harport; anchor in the southwest corner in 4m. Drying rocks lie ¼ cable off the south point of the entrance. No fish farm reported in 2010, some moorings, but space to anchor.

Rounding Ru Hunish, Skye

Northwest coast of Skye from Neist Point to Rubha Hunish

The northwest coast of Skye is deeply indented, withextensive groups of lochs between Dunvegan Head and Waternish Point and the west side of Trotternish. There are no hidden dangers on a direct passage between Neist Point and Rubha Hunish.

A Traffic Separation Scheme exists off Neist Point with related IMO. Recommended Tracks at the northeast end of the Little Minch. The northeast-bound route follows the east side of the Little Minch; in spite of IMO recommendations a number of laden tankers of more than 10,000 tonnes use this passage.

Comet Rock, on the northwest side of the northeast-bound track, is marked by a port-hand light buoy. 1½M northwest of Eilean Trodday.

S card light buoy, south of Eugenie Rock, two miles north-northwest of Fladda-chuain, in place of Sgeir Graidach unlit beacon, which was destroyed.

⊕ One mile WNW of Waternish Point 57°37'·3N 6°39'·2W

Charts

1795 (1:100,000), OS Landranger map 23

Tides

Tides at Neist Point are described on page 51.
Between Neist Point and Ru Bornesketaig, six miles southwest of the north end of Skye, streams run at up to 1½ kns.
The north-going stream begins –0405 Ullapool (+0400 Dover).
The south-going stream begins +0220 Ullapool (–0200 Dover).
At Waternish Point the tide turns 15 minutes later and runs at 2½ kns. Overfalls occur off Waternish Point.

Dangers and marks

Dunvegan Head is 310m high with cliffs on its northwest side sloping down to the north.

A conspicuous radio mast stands three miles south of the head.

Waternish Point is 15m high, with a white light beacon 7m in height at the point.

An t-Iasgair, an islet 21m high, lies 1½ miles north-northwest of Rudha Bornesketaig.

Lights

Neist Point Fl.5s43m16M
An t-Iasgair Fl.6s23m9M
Eugenie Rock light buoy Q(6)+L.Fl.15s
Waternish Point Fl.20s21m8M
Eilean Trodday Fl(2)WRG.10s49m12-9M

Shelter

Loch Dunvegan, Loch Snizort, Duntulm Bay (limited).

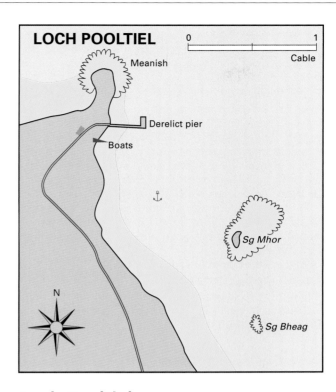

Loch Pooltiel

57°28′N 6°45′W

Exposed northwest, but in moderate weather small boats can anchor between the pier at Meanish on the west side of the loch, and Sgeir Mor, a broad drying rock one cable southeast of the pier.

A rock with less than 2m depth lies about 1¼ cable northwest of the pier.

The bottom appears to consist of boulders.

Small-boat moorings lie southeast of the pier.

The head of the loch has been found to have good holding in firm mud, 3–5m, but dries off for several cables.

Many fishing floats and fish cages lie in the loch.

Supplies

Shop, licensed restaurant, Post Office, telephone, at Glendale at head of the loch. Telephone at Milovaig, up hill from pier. A working water mill may be visited at Glendale.

Loch More, Loch Dunvegan (Colbost)

Loch Dunvegan

57°30′N 6°40′W

Charts

2533 (1:25,000), OS Landranger map 23, OS Explorer map 407

Tides

Constant –0045 Ullapool (–0505 Dover)
Height in metres

MHWS	MHWN	MTL	MLWN	MLWS
5·2	3·8	2·9	1·1	0·7

Dangers and marks

Groban na Sgeire is the peninsula which separates Loch Dunvegan from Loch Bay.

A drying reef extends more than two cables south-southwest from Lampay Islands, two cables west of Groban na Sgeire. Ard Mor open west of Isay, bearing 360° astern, leads clear of this reef.

Fishing floats are scattered throughout Loch Dunvegan.

2½ miles south-southeast of Lampay the channel is reduced to two cables between Fiadhairt, a peninsula on its northeast side, and Eilean Grianal 7m high, with a line of rocks on the southwest side.

Uiginish Point, a mile southeast of Fiadhairt Point, has a white light beacon 5m in height at its end.

A white church tower at Dunvegan village in line with the northwest side of Uiginish Point bearing 128° leads along the middle of the channel.

A G conical light buoy south of Gairbh Eilean lies on the north side of Bo na Famachd over which the depth is 0·9m; if passing southwest of it keep closer to the shore than to the buoy.

A Y light buoy northwest of the pier marks a sewer outfall and has no navigational significance.

Lights

Uiginish Point Fl.WG.3s14m7/5M (white 128°-306° but obscured by Fiadhairt Point when bearing more than 148°).
Bo na Famachd light buoy Fl.G.5s
Outfall buoy Fl.Y.5s
Pier head 2F.R(vert)occas

At night

Keep in the white sector of Uiginish Point light, after which the lights of the village and pier are the only guides.

Dunvegan

The pier has been restored and is usable; dues are charged.

Visitors' moorings have been laid between the pier and the church.

If not using a mooring, anchor abreast of the church clear of moorings.

The bottom between the pier and the moorings is very soft and beyond the hotel it is too shallow for most yachts, but good anchorage can be found there and *Thomasina* (11m c/b yawl) has ridden out a succession of summer gales there.

Supplies at Dunvegan

Shops (including greengrocer, butcher and baker), Post Office, telephone, hotels and restaurants.

Petrol and diesel at garages; gas and gas fittings at garage. DIY/builders' merchant. Launderette at caravan site.

Gaeltec, an electronics firm, may be willing to help with electronic repairs and light machining in emergencies.

Diver at Stein ☎ 01470 592219, marine engineer at Uig ☎ 01470 542300.

Other anchorages

Gairbh Eilean Anchor between the castle and the island clear of rocks above water and drying which lie further north.

Loch More, 57°27'N 6°38'W, behind Eilean Dubh Beag off the southwest shore.

Clach a' Charra on the northwest side of the entrance is marked by a red perch with a T-shaped head, and rarely covers.

Below half tide a drying rock southwest of Eilean Dubh Beag will be visible, and better shelter can then be found east-southeast of the slip at Colbost.

Permanent moorings are laid in Loch More and Loch Erghallen, and an area south-southeast of Eilean Dubh Beag has been allocated for anchorage by visitors.

Restaurant one mile south from slip.

Loch Erghallan, 57°26'N 6°37'W. Keep on the 128° line until within a cable of Uiginish Point to avoid Bo Channanich; turn to starboard and anchor not more than a cable south of Eilean Mor.

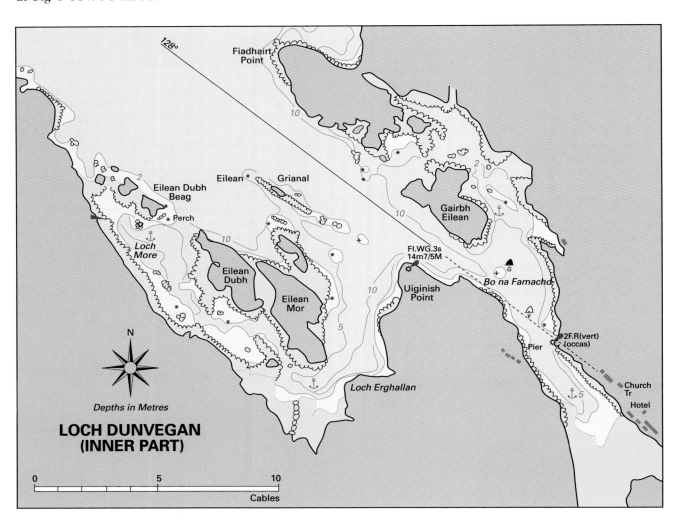

LOCH DUNVEGAN
(INNER PART)

Depths in Metres

Loch Bay

57°30'·5N 6°35'W

Tides *as Loch Dunvegan on page 55*

Dangers and marks

Three islands, Isay, Mingay and Clett, lie in the entrance to the loch.

The passage north of Clett is ¾ mile wide but Sgeir a' Chuain, which dries, extends ¼ mile north of Isay.

To clear Sgeir a Chuain, keep a mobile phone mast on Beinn na Mointeich bearing <085° to lead clear of Isay reef.

Several drying rocks lie south of Isay with a passage two cables wide south of them.

A spit with a depth of 2·4m extending 1½ cables north of Groban na Sgeire at the south side of the entrance may cause momentary alarm.

If approaching Loch Bay by the south of Isay, keep Dunvegan Head bearing 280° astern and follow the south shore of the passage until the west side of Ardmore Point is open east of Mingay 338°.

Sgeir nam Biast, a reef two cables across, part of which is above water, lies ¾ mile east of the south end of Isay and ½ mile from the south shore.

Groups of shellfish lines are moored east of Isay and Mingay, and in Lovaig Bay.

Anchorages

Isay, between Isay and Mingay.

From north approach with the east side of Rubha Maol showing between Mingay and Clett 128° to clear Sgeir a' Chuain, or Waternish Hall open of Clett 090° as above, and turn in to the channel between the islands when the big ruined house on Isay is visible.

From south approach with the west side of Ardmore Point open east of Mingay 338° to clear the east side of rocks south of Isay.

Anchor between Isay and the south end of Mingay. May be lumpy with wind from north or south.

Ardmore Bay, at the north end of Loch Bay is well sheltered from north, but the holding is said to be poor; the west side of the bay is shoal.

Stein, on the east shore of the southeast part of the loch, south-southeast of the pier.

There are many local boats on moorings, as well as visitors' moorings.

Apart from the obvious westerly exposure, there is sufficient fetch to make this a very uncomfortable anchorage in strong south winds.

At the head of the loch there is space to anchor sheltered from southerly gales, in spite of fish cages moored there.

Supplies at Stein

Pub, restaurant. Water; ask at Lochbay Restaurant, next to Stein Inn. Shop, Post Office, telephone ¾ mile uphill. Diver ℡ 01470 592219.

Loch Snizort

57°35'N 6°30'W

Charts

1795 (1:100,000), 2533 (1:25,000)
OS map Landranger 23, OS Explorer map 408

Tides

Constant –0030 Ullapool (–0450 Dover)
Height in metres

MHWS	MHWN	MTL	MLWN	MLWS
5·3	3·5	2·1	1·9	0·7

Ascrib Islands

These islands, 1¼ miles from the west side of the loch, are generally clean, but drying and submerged rocks extend 1¾ cables northwest of the southwest point of South Ascrib.

Very occasional anchorage may be found in the bight on the west side of Eilean Garave, where the bottom is sand outwith the 2m line.

A shallow landlocked pool lies northwest of the house on South Ascrib, and a shoal-draught boat might lie there at neaps with lines ashore.

Dangers

See approach to individual anchorages.

Lights

Waternish Point Fl.20s21m8M
Uig Pier head Iso.WRG.4s9m7-4M

Anchorages

Aros Bay, 57°33'N 6°33'W, an open bay on the west side of the loch where, formerly, car ferries used to shelter when the weather was too wild for them to approach Uig.

Loch Diubaig, 57°30'N 6°27'·5W, occasional anchorage in an open bay in the southwest corner of Loch Snizort. Bottom sand with patches of weed.

Loch Greshornish, 57°30'N 6°26'W, gives the best shelter in Loch Snizort.

Drying rocks lie one cable west of the south end of Eilean Mor at the entrance, as well as 1½ cables north of Greshornish Point, the west side of the entrance, and ½ cable off the east side of Greshornish Point.

The clear passage west of Eilean Mor is ½ mile wide; the passage east of Eilean Mor is three cables wide with no hazards.

Large unlit fish cages lie at the mouth of the loch, and many shellfish lines obstruct most of the head.

Submerged and drying rocks lie ¾ cable from the east shore two miles south of Greshornish Point.

The east tangent of Greshornish Point in line with the west side of Eilean Mor 018° leads west of these rocks.

Shop, pub and swimming pool at Edinbane on the east shore.

Loch Snizort Beag, 57°29'N 6°20'W, gives some shelter three miles from its mouth, just within the middle arm, the head of which dries off for one mile.

A submerged rock, Beatson, at a depth of 1·2m lies near the east shore of the loch 1½ miles from the mouth.

Hotel at the head of the middle arm.

Loch Treaslane, the western arm, is also sheltered although the head also dries off for four cables, and both these branches have good holding on mud. Loch Eyre, the eastern arm, dries off completely.

Christie Rocks which dry 2·2m lie 1½ cables offshore, about a mile south of the south point of Uig Bay. Stack of Skudiburgh, ¾ mile north of Uig Bay, open of the land 360°, leads clear of these rocks.

Poll na h-Ealaidh, a small inlet southeast of Christie Rocks, provides some shelter in offshore winds.

Uig Pier

Uig Bay

57°34'·5N 6°23'W

The terminal for the ferry to Harris and North Uist.

The long pier provides some shelter, but much of the bay inshore of it dries.

The pier is used by fishing boats morning and evening and it is not recommended for yachts to lie there overnight, although they can go alongside during the day. Visitors' moorings (three) east of pier.

At night

Approach in the white sector of the light at the pier and keep a good lookout for fishing boats.

Supplies

Petrol and diesel from garage at pier. Shop at pier, larger shop with Post Office at head of the loch. Telephone at pier. Hotels.

Marine engineer and fishermen's chandlery, Sandy Morrison ☎ 01470 542300.

An ATM is located inside the CalMac waiting rooms at the ferry terminal and can be accessed during normal port opening hours.

Other anchorages

Camas Beag on the south side of Uig Bay is an alternative anchorage in southerly winds but is deep until close to the head.

Tulm Bay (Duntulm)

57°41'N 6°21'W

Charts

1795 (1:100,000), also on *2210* (1:50,000)
OS map Landranger 23, OS Explorer maps *390*, for Ardnamurchan, and *398*, for Sound of Arisaig northward.

Tides

Off Rubha Hunish the spring rate is 3kns

The northeast-going stream begins –0405 Ullapool (+0400 Dover)

The southwest-going stream begins +0220 Ullapool (–0200 Dover)

Constant –0030 Ullapool (–0450 Dover)

Height in metres

MHWS	MHWN	MTL	MLWN	MLWS
5·3	3·5	3·1	1·9	0·7

Marks

A lattice-work communications tower stands on Cnoc Roll southeast of the bay.

An t-Iasgair, 22m high, lies 1½ miles offshore north-northwest of Ru Bornesketaig.

Tulm Island lies in the middle of the bay and the ruins of Duntulm Castle stand on Ru Meanish at the south point of the bay.

Dangers

A drying reef extends about ½ cable southeast from the south end of Tulm Island, and drying reefs extend ½ cable west and northwest from Ru Meanish on Skye.

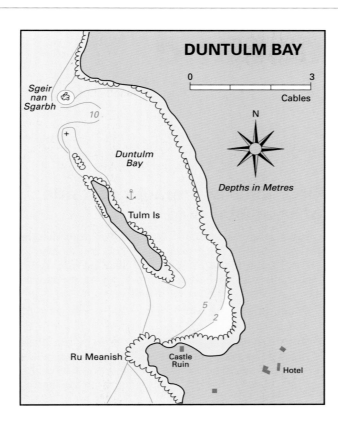

DUNTULM BAY

Sgeir nan Sgarbh

10

Duntulm Bay

Tulm Is

5

2

Ru Meanish

Castle Ruin

Hotel

0 — 3 Cables

N

Depths in Metres

At the north end of Tulm Island a reef partly drying and partly submerged extends 1¼ cables north-northwest.

Sgeir nan Sgarbh which dries 4·6m lies near the Skye shore, with a narrow channel on either side of it.

A detached rock drying at LW lies just off the reef northeast of Sgeir nan Sgarbh.

Directions

Approach by the south entrance keeping midway between Tulm Island and Skye, heading 090° until the northeast side of Tulm Island is open.

From north, if Sgeir nan Sgarbh is visible either between the rock and the Skye shore – keeping rather closer to the rock – or ¼–½ cable south of the rock.

Anchor close to the northeast side of Tulm Island, north of the mid-point of the island, but this may be uncomfortable, as the tide may hold a yacht across the wind.

The bottom consists of sand with patches of weed.

A strong eddy is felt in the south part of the bay with south-going tides.

Services

Hotel.

Tulm Bay

IV. Sound of Sleat and Loch Alsh

The Sound of Sleat and lochs on the mainland side are completely sheltered from the open sea, but surrounded by mountains and subject to severe squalls.

Charts

2208 (1:50,000)
OS *Landranger map 33*, OS *Explorer map 413*

Tides

The northeast-going stream begins +0550 Ullapool (+0130 Dover).

The southwest-going stream begins –0010 Ullapool (–0430 Dover).

Dangers

On the Skye side of the sound, rocks above water and drying lie up to two cables offshore southeast and south of Armadale.

Tartar Rock, four miles north-northeast of Armadale with a depth of 1·5m, lies two cables offshore.

Off the mainland shore, submerged and drying rocks lie up to two cables north-northeast of Airor Island and, at the mouth of Glen Ghuserein, 1½ miles northwest of Airor, a bank dries off ¼ mile from the shore.

Conspicuous marks

Mallaig village at the southeast point of the entrance to the sound.

Armadale Pier, with a white building on its head.

Sandaig Island light beacon (north of Loch Hourn entrance) 12m high.

Isle Ornsay light tower, white, 18m high.

Lights

Sgeir Dhearg, Mallaig Fl(2)WG.8s6m5M
Mallaig Steamer Pier Iso.WRG.4s6m9–6M
Armadale Pier Oc.R.6s6m6M (not easily seen among shore lights)
Isle Ornsay Oc.8s18m15M 157°-vis-030°
Isle Ornsay north Fl.R.6s8m4M
Sandaig Island light beacon Fl.6s12m8M

At night

To clear dangers off Armadale keep Isle Ornsay light in sight bearing not more than 030°; to clear Tartar Rock, keep this light bearing not more than 025°.

To clear the land north of Loch Nevis keep the white sector of Sgeir Dhearg light at Mallaig in sight.

Shelter

Limited at: Glaschoille (Loch Nevis), Armadale, Isle Ornsay.

Occasional anchorages east side of Sleat Peninsula

Camas Daraich, 57°01′N 6°00′W, lies immediately east of Point of Sleat with a sandy beach at its head.

A rock more than a cable from the west side of the bay dries at about half tide with a drying reef north of it and other drying rocks southwest.

Port na Long is a more open bay a mile east of Camas Daraich.

Acairseid an Rudha on the west side of the Sleat peninsula seven cables north of the light beacon has a jetty and leading beacons, originally for servicing the light, but is probably best visited from the land.

Thomasina at Camas Daraich

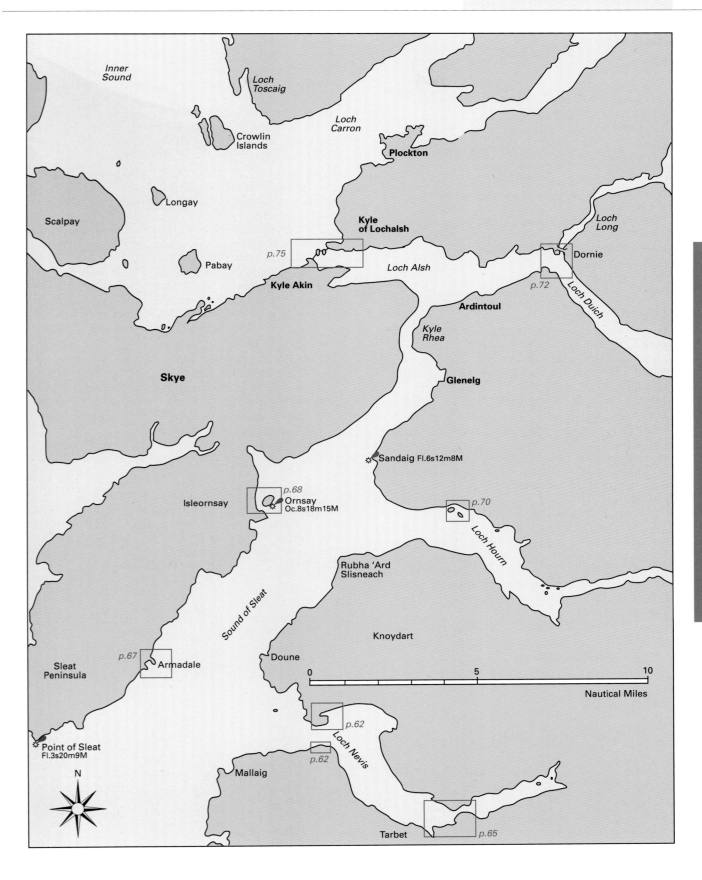

Inner
Sound

Loch
Toscaig

Crowlin
Islands

Loch
Carron

Plockton

Longay

Scalpay

Pabay

**Kyle
of Lochalsh**

p.75

Loch Alsh

Loch
Long

Dornie

p.72

Loch
Duich

Kyle Akin

Ardintoul

Kyle
Rhea

Skye

Glenelg

Sandaig Fl.6s12m8M

Isleornsay

p.68

Ornsay
Oc.8s18m15M

p.70

Loch Hourn

Rubha 'Ard
Slisneach

Knoydart

Doune

Sound of Sleat

p.67

Armadale

Sleat
Peninsula

0   5   10

Nautical Miles

Point of Sleat
Fl.3s20m9M

N

p.62

Loch Nevis

p.62

Mallaig

Tarbet

p.65

Loch Nevis

⊕ ¼M south of 1·2m rock 57°01'·3N 5°44'·7W

Charts

2541 (1:25,000), *1987* and later editions only
OS *map Landranger 33*

Tides

Streams in the entrance south of Rubha Raonuill run at ½kn; elsewhere they are weak except at the narrows where they run at 3kns.

The in-going stream begins +0530 Ullapool (+0110 Dover)

The out-going stream begins –0050 Ullapool (–0510 Dover)

Constant –0040 Ullapool (–0500 Dover)

Height in metres

MHWS	MHWN	MTL	MLWN	MLWS
5·0	3·8	2·9	2·0	0·7

Dangers and marks

A white monumental statue stands near the southeast point of Rubha Raonuill.

Rocks, above water and drying, lie on the N side of the entrance between Eilean Glas and Rubha Raonuill.

Bogha cas Sruth which dries 1·8m, 3½ cables west-southwest of Rubha Raonuill, is the most dangerous. Inverie House just showing south of Rubha Raonuill 083° leads one cable south of Bogha cas Sruth.

A submerged rock lies more than a cable south-southwest of Rubha Raonuill at a depth of 1·2m; the beacon on Bogha Don in line with Inverie Church 075° leads close south of this rock.

Bogha Don, a drying rock 1½ cables southeast of Rubha Raonuill is marked by a tapered stone beacon with a cross topmark

On the south side of the loch, Bo Ruag dries 3m, ¾ cable offshore and about three cables west of Rubha na Moine, the point where the shore turns sharply to the south.

Anchorages

Port Giubhais, 57°01'N 5°44'·3W, on the east side of Eilean Giubhais provides occasional anchorage for small boats under a steep hillside on the south side of the loch.

Drying reefs extend northeast of Eilean Giubhais and a detached rock dries 1·2m northwest of Eilean Giubhais; Bo Ruag, described above, lies one cable east-northeast of the mouth of the inlet.

Glaschoille, 57°02'N 5°43'W, is particularly suitable in northerly winds to which Mallaig is exposed.

Sgeirean Glasa is marked by a slim pole which is not easily seen at HW.

Drying reefs extend about ¼ cable northwest and southeast of Sgeirean Glasa beacon and other rocks lie further inshore.

The bay south of Glaschoille House and east of Eilean na Glaschoille is occupied by workboats on moorings, but space can usually be found to anchor among them. The bottom falls away steeply ½ cable from the low water line. The seabed is sand and mud with some dense weed patches.

Inverie, 57°02'N 5°41'W, is in the northeast corner of the outer loch.

Anchor clear of moorings and the approach to the pier, but the holding is poor.

Visitors' moorings are available by arrangement with either the pub or Pier House.

The old pier has been demolished and a new pier, with a ferry ramp and steps, built about 150m northwest, with lights at its head 2FR(vert).

Services and Supplies

Shop, Post Office three days a week at ferry times only. Note there are no facilities for rubbish disposal. Telephone, water, *Calor Gas*, pub/restaurant, showers at pub, ferry to Mallaig. Meals also at The Pier House if booked in advance.

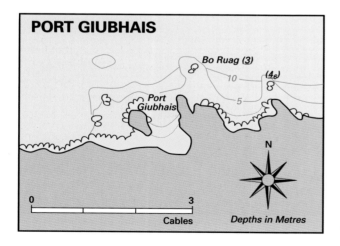

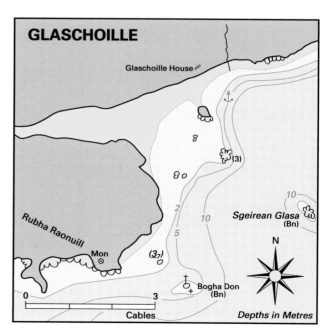

Glaschoille

Inverie; new pier and ferry terminal *Patrick Roach*

Eilean Giubhais, looking towards Rudha Raonuill

Tarbet Bay, 56°58'·3N 5°38'W, on the south shore near the west end of the narrows.

Green huts belonging to an adventure centre stand on the shore of a bay west of Ardintigh Point, ½ mile west of Tarbet Bay, and a wooden house stands on

Torr an Albannaich, the east point of the bay, with a flagstaff on an islet off the point; a drying rock lies ¼ cable west of the islet.

The relatively shallow area at the mouth of the bay is found to have a bottom of rock and kelp with doubtful holding. Much of the bay occupied by permanent moorings.

It is liable to be very squally, especially in southerly winds.

Loch Nevis Narrows, 56°59'N 5°37'W, is entered eastward of Torr an Albannaich (*see above*).

Roinn a' Chaolais, a long shoal spit, extends southwest from the north point of the entrance to the narrows and there are various drying rocks in and beyond the narrows.

Tidal streams run at 3kns, turning as above.

Steer for the north side of Torr an Albannaich and when ½ cable from the shore steer for a white cottage on the south shore beyond Kylesmorar 065°.

Alter course again to keep in mid-channel at the beginning of the narrows, closing the north shore beyond the white cottage to avoid Sgeir an t-Sruith and a drying spit at the east end of the south side of the channel.

A shoal rock on the north side, three cables beyond the east end of the narrows is avoided by keeping Kylesknoydart cottage open south of the north point at the east end of the narrows 257°.

Drying rocks lie up to a cable off either shore.

At the head of the loch anchor either north or southeast of Eilean Maol as convenient clear of any moorings; the head of the loch dries for ½ mile.

A new jetty has been built in the bay ½ mile west of Eilean Maol.

Loch Nevis Narrows, with Tarbet Bay on the right

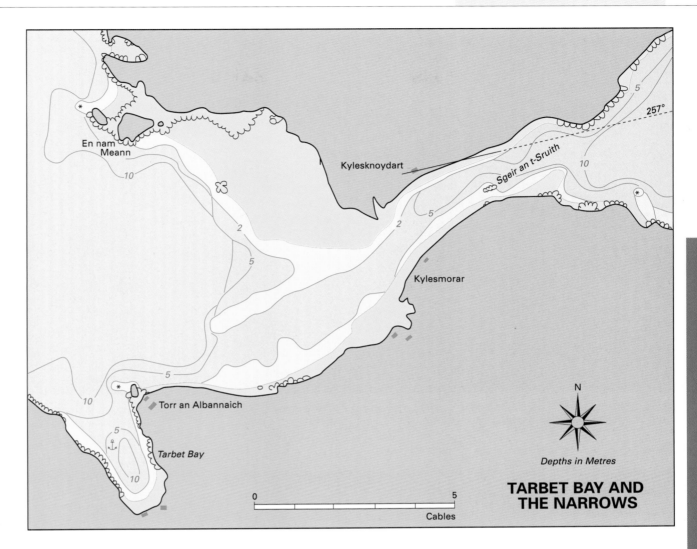

TARBET BAY AND THE NARROWS

Depths in Metres

Occasional anchorages in the Sound of Sleat

Sandaig Bay, 57°02′·5N 5°46′W, is an attractive daytime stop northeast of Glas Eilean at the mouth of Loch Nevis.

If coming from Loch Nevis the rocks on the east side should be carefully studied.

Sandaig Bay, Sound of Sleat

At the head of the bay a rock dries at half tide about a cable southeast of the islet there.

Doune (Dun Bane Bay), 57°04′N 5°47′·3W, a bay facing northwest a couple of miles north of Loch Nevis entrance.

Visitors' moorings are laid on the southwest side of the bay, sheltered from southwest by An Fraochag. The east side of the bay is shoal inshore.

Services

Meals (booking requested by 1700), showers, telephone, metfax, diver, repairs.

Water and diesel at the stone jetty on north side of promontory north of moorings; ask at house before going alongside.

☎ 01687 462667.

Airor, 57°05′N 5°46′W, a shallow bay a mile northeast of Doune Bay, best visited at neaps or with a very shallow-draught boat.

The entrance between the island and a reef off the south point is only ½ cable wide and submerged rocks extend ½ cable southwest from the island.

Doune Bay: visitors' moorings at the right; note shoal ground at the head of the right-hand bay. Fuel jetty at south side of left-hand bay

Airor Island

Armadale

⊕ ¼ mile north-northeast of Eilean Mhaol 57°03′·8N 5°53′W

Tides
Constant −0040 Ullapool (−0500 Dover)
Height in metres

MHWS	MHWN	MTL	MLWN	MLWS
5·0	3·8	2·9	2·0	0·7

Dangers and marks
Eilean Maol, 3m high, is the outermost of a group of rocks east of Ardvasar Promontory (Rubha Phoil), south-southeast of Armadale Pier.

A detached rock dries ½ cable north-northeast of Eilean Maol; the north-northeast face of the pier open leads clear of the detached rock.

Anchorage
Visitors' moorings lie northeast of the old jetty. *Note* Contributions are invited for the upkeep of the visitors' moorings at the pontoon on the inner side of the old pier (£10/night). Together with Isle of Skye Yachts (formerly Sleat Marine Services) moorings these leave little room for anchoring, but the bottom is firm sand.

It may be possible to leave a yacht in the care of Isle of Skye Yachts.

The bay is exposed to seas from northeast and in these conditions Knock Bay (*see below*) may be more comfortable.

A roll-on ferry terminal stands at the north end of the Steamer Pier.

Lights
Armadale pier head shows Oc.R.6s6m6M, but is not easily picked out among the shore lights.

Armadale. Leave plenty of space for the ferry to manoeuvre. Water and fuel at stone jetty on north side

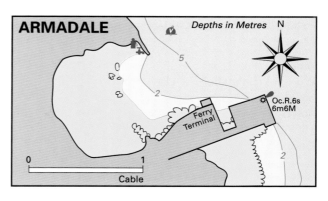

At night
When approaching from southwest, keep Isle Ornsay light in sight to clear Eilean Maol.

Services and supplies
Shop, hotel at Ardvasar (one mile south), café, bar, takeaway and camping shop at pier. Doctor and district nurse.

Water supply at the north pier is metered and locked; key from Isle of Skye Yachts during working hours. The access is easy from the pontoon. Isle of Skye Yachts supply fuel and water at the moorings. There is also a water supply from a stand pipe, and skips for rubbish, at the ferry bus park on the south side of the bay. Diesel, emergency repairs to hull, engine and sails, and some chandlery, from Isle of Skye Yachts ☎ 01471 844216.

Other anchorages
Knock Bay, three miles north-north-east of Armadale; the holding is said to be bad and the west side of the bay foul; the depth decreases suddenly from 18–1m.

Camas Croise, 57°08′N 5°48′W, has a bottom of stiff clay.

IV. SOUND OF SLEAT AND LOCH ALSH

SKYE AND NORTHWEST SCOTLAND **67**

Isleornsay Harbour

57°08'·8N 5°47'·7W

Tides

Constant −0050 Ullapool (−0510 Dover)

Height in metres

MHWS	MHWN	MTL	MLWN	MLWS
4·8	3·7	2·7	1·6	0·7

Dangers and marks

A white lighthouse, 19m high, stands on Eilean Sionnach, a tidal islet southeast of Ornsay.

A grey stone light beacon stands on the northeast side of a reef off the north end of Ornsay, but part of the reef extends northwest of the beacon. Give the north shore of Ornsay a berth of at least a cable.

The bay shoals gradually towards its head and dries about a cable short of the pier.

Lights

Ornsay lighthouse Oc.8s18m15M
Ornsay Island light beacon Fl.R.6s8m4M
Pier head 2F.R(vert) and floodlights

Anchorages

There is said now to be little fishing boat traffic, but a good anchor light should be shown. Salmon nets may be encountered on the west side of the bay.

Anchorage off Duisdale Hotel at the west side of the entrance is more out of the way and said to be more sheltered, as well as being a shorter distance to row ashore.

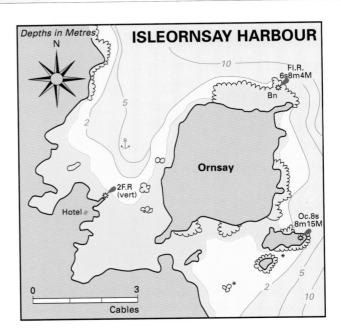

ISLEORNSAY HARBOUR

A bay on the west side, below a conspicuous church has been found to provide good holding in a southerly gale, with no weed.

Both Duisdale House Hotel and Kinloch House Hotel in Loch na Dal, a mile north of Isle Oronsay, provide visitors' moorings for their customers.

Isleornsay

Ornsay lighthouse

Supplies

Hotel by the pier. Post Office, water tap. Baths at Duisdale Hotel.

Other anchorages

Loch na Dal, 57°10′N 5°47′W, is a better anchorage in northerly winds.

Sgeir Ghobhlach stands above water on a coastal reef ¾ cable offshore on the north side of the entrance to Loch na Dal.

Detached rocks, both drying and submerged, lie more than a cable from the shore in places up to two miles northeast of Sgeir Ghobhlach.

Eilean Rarsaidh Anna Lawrence

Loch Hourn

57°08′N 5°40′W

One of the most spectacular lochs in Scotland but subject to very high rainfall and severe squalls.

Charts

2541 (1:25,000)
OS map Landranger 33

Tides

The in-going stream begins –0610 Ullapool (+0155 Dover)
The out-going stream begins +0005 Ullapool (–0415 Dover)
Streams run at 3kns in narrows east of Corr Eileanan, with an eddy on the flood on the south side of the inner loch, but they are weak in the outer loch.
Constant –0110 Ullapool (–0530 Dover)

Height in metres

MHWS	MHWN	MTL	MLWN	MLWS
5·0	3·8	2·9	2·0	0·8

Dangers and marks

Sgeir Ulibhe, in the entrance of the loch about one-third of the width from the north side, dries 2·1m, with the remains of a metal beacon on it, and a rock just submerged lies a cable west of Sgeir Ulibhe.

Clansman Rock, halfway between Sgeir Ulibhe and the north shore, has a depth of only 2·1m over it.

Anchorages

Eilean Rarsaidh, 57°09′N 5°37′W, on the north shore of the outer loch has several drying rocks as on the plan which are not correctly shown on older copies of chart *2541*.

Anchor north or east of Eilean Rarsaidh. Shelter is said to be better than would appear from the chart and it is often preferred to Isleornsay.

Eilean Rarsaidh. A further rock is reported to lie between the two rocks which are just showing near the mainland shore

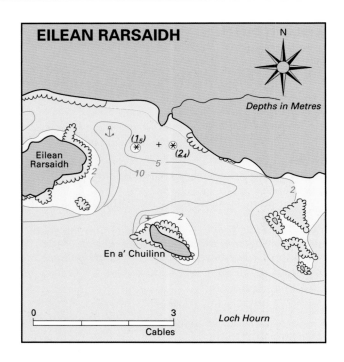

EILEAN RARSAIDH

N

Depths in Metres

Eilean
Rarsaidh

En a' Chuilinn

0   3
Cables

Loch Hourn

Loch Hourn Beag. The scale is deceptive and the channel is
only a few metres wide

Camas Ban, 57°08'N 5°34'W, Arnisdale. The bay is
reported to be completely obstructed by moorings.

Eilean a' Phiobaire, 57°07'N 5°35'W. The passage
and anchorage are reported to be completely
blocked by a fish farm.

Poll a' Mhuineil, 57°06'N 5°34'W, is deep until close
to the head of the pool and subject to severe squalls
from south.

Loch Hourn Beag

57°06'·6N 5°24'W

The upper part of Loch Hourn is reached through a
sequence of narrow passages east of Corr Eileanan.

The head of Barrisdale Bay, south of Corr
Eileanan, dries up to half a mile.

Ellice Shoal lies four cables west of the two
southern Corr Eileanan, and Duncan Shoal lies two
cables west of the north Corr Eilean.

The tide runs at 3kns through the narrows east of
Corr Eileanan.

The main passage lies south of Corr Eileanan, and
the southwest shore should be kept between ¼-½ mile
until the south point of the first narrows is open
south of the south Corr Eilean.

Pass within two cables south of the south island
and then steer to pass within a cable south of Eilean
a' Gharb-Iain to avoid an extensive bank which dries
off the south shore.

The passage between the north and middle Corr Eileanan is clean but the south side of Eilean a' Gharb-Iain must be kept in sight in the passage 085° to avoid Duncan and Ellice Shoals.

At Caolas Mor, 1¼ miles east of Corr Eileanan, the south shore should be kept ½ cable off to avoid an extensive bank which dries southwest of the promontory on the north side of the narrows.

At Eilean Mousker (Mhogh-sgeir), just over a mile east-northeast of Caolas Mor, the passage is south of the island, keeping closer to the island to avoid a drying bank off the south shore.

Island Rock, ½ cable east of the island, covers at half tide.

Caolas an Loch Bhig, 1¼ miles further east, leads to Loch Beag.

The channel winds around and is only 0·6m deep, but if the passage is taken on the last two hours of the flood it should present little problem.

When you can see clear water through the middle of the entrance there is 2·4m in the channel.

At this time Island Rock, east of Eilean Mhogh-sgeir, is just covered, around half tide.

After passing the cottage at Skiary on the south shore outside the narrows, close the south shore when a ruined shed is abeam.

Keep about 20m from the south shore until you come to a weed-covered spit with two rocks on the shore above it; follow closely the edge of the spit until on a line between the two rocks and the west end of the beach on the north shore.

Follow close to the north shore and then along the edge of the shingle spit which extends from the north shore, until more than midway across the channel again and then make for the middle of Loch Beag.

The tidal stream runs at about 2kns and tends to set a yacht off course.

Holding in Loch Beag is poor and the head of the loch dries out to a line from the steps on the south side to the ruins of a boathouse on the north side. In a westerly gale the best shelter is in a bight of the north shore north of Eilean Mhogh-sgeir.

Sandaig Bay

57°10'N 5°41'·5W

Lies 1½ miles north of the entrance to Loch Hourn (not to be confused with the bay of the same name north of the entrance to Loch Nevis) southeast of Sandaig Islands, on the northwest point of which is a light beacon.

Rocks, submerged and drying, lie up to 1½ cables southeast of the islands, and off Sgeir nan Eun the most southerly above-water rock.

A drying reef extends about a cable from Rubha Mor at the southeast point of the bay.

Good shelter in winds with any northerly component.

Glenelg Boat Harbour *Anna Lawrence*

Glenelg

57°12'·5N 5°38'W

On the east shore of Sound of Sleat, a mile southeast of the entrance to Kyle Rhea.

A monument stands on Rubha Mhic Cuinn and a submerged rock lies a cable west of Rubha Mhic Cuinn.

A wooden jetty lies a cable south of the promontory.

Anchor southwest of the jetty (the head of which covers at HW) clear of moorings, but the holding is poor.

A small pool, the entrance to which dries, where local boats are moored, lies north of the promontory.

Supplies

At Glenelg, ½ mile from the jetty: shop, Post Office, *Calor Gas*, petrol, hotel.

Kyle Rhea and Loch Alsh

Charts

2540 (1:20,000)
OS map Landranger 33, OS Explorer map 413

Tides

Tidal streams in Kyle Rhea run at up to 8kns and possibly more on occasions, with eddies along both sides; during the second half of the flood tide (north-going) the stream sets onto rocks on the west side of the channel.

At the south entrance to the kyle a southerly wind and ebb tide set up dangerous overfalls.

An eddy forms in Bernera Bay southeast of the south entrance on the south-going tide.

During the second half of the flood the stream sets across rocks on the west shore which are covered.

The stream runs at its fastest in the south entrance to the kyle.

The north-going stream begins +0600 Ullapool (+0140 Dover)

The south-going stream begins at HW Ullapool (–0420 Dover)

Dangers and marks

Drying rocks extend up to ¾ cable off both shores of Kyle Rhea.

A light beacon stands on the west shore of the kyle.

Sgeir na Caillich, nearly two cables north of the west point of the north entrance, is marked by a concrete pillar 2m in height.

Directions

Keep in mid-channel. If tacking beware eddies inshore.

Coming south, if the wind is southerly, beware overfalls ½ mile south of the entrance near the west shore. The worst can be avoided by steering for the southeast shore until clear south of a line between Dunan Ruadh and Glenelg village.

Anchorages

To wait for the tide at the south end, anchor off the jetty at Glenelg (*see above*) or on the west shore, north of a cable beacon standing 3½ cables south of the mouth of Kylerhea River. A drying bank extends nearly two cables from the river mouth.

At the north end anchor not less than 1½ cable west-northwest of Sgeir na Caillich beacon to avoid submerged rocks (although, with the large-scale chart, space can be found closer to the shore).

Lights

Kyle Rhea light beacon Fl.WRG.3s7m11–8M
Sgeir na Caillich light beacon Fl(2)R.6s3m4M

At night

The white sectors of Kyle Rhea light beacon lead through the entrances to the kyle.

Supplies

At Glenelg (*see page 71*).

East Loch Alsh and Loch Duich

Charts

2541 (1:25,000 and 1:12,500)
OS map Landranger 33

Tides in East Loch Alsh

The in-going stream begins –0610 Ullapool (+0155 Dover)

The out-going stream begins –0005 Ullapool (–0425 Dover)

Constant –0025 Ullapool (–0445 Dover)

Height in metres

MHWS	MHWN	MTL	MLWN	MLWS
5·3	3·8	3·0	2·1	0·7

Dangers and marks

Glas Eilean, 6m high with extensive drying banks all round it, lies in the middle of the entrance to the east part of Loch Alsh.

In the channel to the north of Glas Eilean, Racoon Rock, at a depth of 1·8m, is marked by a green conical light buoy on its northwest side.

Rocks awash and drying extend more than ½ cable from the shore northwest of Racoon Rock leaving less than a cable between them and the buoy.

Slioch G con light buoy lies a cable north-northwest of Glas Eilean.

A detached drying reef lies four cables east of the north part of Glas Eilean.

The channel south of Glas Eilean has drying banks on both sides extending up to 1½ cables in places.

In the approach from west a drying bank extends a cable north of Ardintoul Point.

A submerged rock lies more than a cable east of Glas Eilean on the north side of the channel.

Do not approach Ardintoul Point to a depth of less than 10m and thereafter keep equidistant between visible shorelines.

The low water lines of Glas Eilean and Ardintoul Point in line lead south of the rock east of Glas Eilean.

Lights in east part of Loch Alsh

Racoon Rock light buoy Fl.5s
Slioch light buoy Fl(3)G.6s

Anchorages

Avernish Bay, north of Glas Eilean, although obstructed by underwater cables, may provide shelter in strong east or northeast winds.

Ardintoul Bay, southwest of Glas Eilean, is occupied by fish cages, but there may be space to anchor inshore of them.

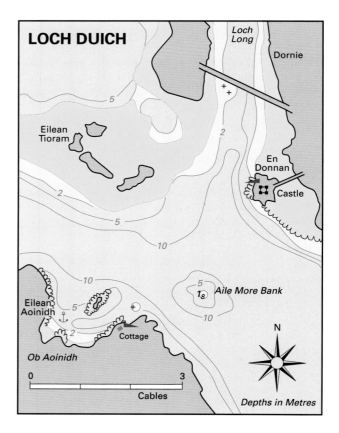

Totaig *Tim Whittome*

Eilean Donan Castle and Loch Long *Tim Whittome*

Loch Duich is entered between Eilean Aoinidh, a rocky wooded point on the south shore, and Eilean Tioram, which is low and grassy, on the north side.

The foreshore of Eilean Tioram dries off two cables on the west side and ¾ cable on other sides.

Loch Duich and the Five Sisters of Kintail. The old ferry house at Totaig is at the right

Aile More Bank at a depth of 1·8m lies in the middle of the loch three cables east of Eilean Aoinidh.

Eilean Donnan Castle is conspicuous on the northeast shore at the east side of the entrance to Loch Long.

Many fish cages are moored off the southwest shore of the loch.

Ob Aoinidh (Totaig), 57°16′N 5°31′·5W, is a small bay on the east side of the peninsula named Eilean Aoinidh.

It is surrounded by trees and an extensive reef partly above water lies in the middle of the bay.

The bottom is rather hard so that an anchor does not dig in easily and the current runs strongly round the bay, apparently continuously anti-clockwise at some states of the tide, at other times clockwise on the flood and anticlockwise with the ebb.

Several moorings restrict anchoring space.

A rocky shelf extends east of the north point of Eilean Aoinidh but further south the west shore of the bay is steep-to and a line can be taken ashore to restrict swinging and hold a yacht out of the worst of the tide.

A rock awash lies less than ¼ cable off the old ferry cottage at the east point of the bay.

Water may be available from a tap at the ferry cottage.

Dornie, 57°17′N 5°31′W, at the mouth of Loch Long northeast of Eilean Aoinidh is an occasional anchorage for buying stores or visiting the castle, but the tide runs strongly into and out from Loch Long. The bridge across the mouth of Loch Long has restricted headroom, about 2·5m. Anchor off a slip on the northwest side of the castle.

Shops, hotels, Post Office, telephone, petrol, gas.

Ratagan Bay, 57°13′·2N 5°26′·5W, southeast of a promontory which lies southeast of Ratagan youth hostel, a prominent white building.

The head of the bay dries out four cables, but on the southwest side a depth of 5m can be found a cable from the shore, and good shelter has been found there.

Invershiel Anchor off a concrete slip by the hotel on the east side of Bay of Invershiel.

Post office, telephone, hotel, petrol and diesel. Baths at hotel. Shop at Shiel Bridge, ¾ mile.

Place names and names of natural features become confusing to a stranger around here. A loch is normally an inlet of water with only one open end; a kyle is a narrow passage between islands, or sometimes a narrow part of a loch, such as Kylestrome. It may be written as *caol*, as in Caol Rona, or *caolas*, as in Caolas Scalpay; in each case it is pronouonced 'kyle' or 'kyles'.

Loch Alsh, however, is an open-ended body of water linking Kyle Rhea and Kyle Akin as well as Loch Duich. Kyle Rhea joins Kyle Akin to the Sound of Sleat, and Kyle Akin joins Loch Alsh to Inner Sound.

The township on the north side of Kyle Akin is Kyle of Lochalsh, and that on the south side is Kyleakin (as a single word).

Collectively the area is known as Kyle, and the harbour office, located at Kyle of Lochalsh, is formally addressed as 'Kyle Harbour'.

Loch Alsh, west part

Chart
2540 (1:20,000)

Dangers and marks
A submerged wreck, two cables off the south shore of Loch Alsh between Kyle Rhea and Kyle Akin, lies north of a group of fish cages, marked by east and west cardinal light buoys.

In Scalpaidh Bay, ½ mile east-northeast of Eileanan Dubha, a rock which dries 0·8m lies more than a cable offshore.

Lights
Sgeir na Caillich light beacon Fl(2)R.6s3m4M
South shore, E card Q(3)10s
South shore, W card Q(9)15s

Anchorages
The following bays on the north side of Loch Alsh have been used for anchoring under appropriate conditions.

Aird a Mhill Bay, 57°16'·5N 5°36'W, provides some shelter in easterly winds but the head of the bay dries off one cable and the bottom drops rapidly to more than 30m. Anchor in 5m just east of the mouth of the burn.

Balmacara Bay, 57°17'N 5°39'W, anchor towards the west side of the bay east of a jetty below trees. The rest of the bay dries off for one cable.

Hotel and pub, shop, *Calor Gas*. Visitors' moorings.

Scalpaidh Bay, 57°17'N 5°41'·5W. Anchor in 5m, sand with weed patches, in the western third of the bay, keeping well clear of the rock referred to above which dries 0·8m.

Loch na Beiste, 57°16'N 5°43'W, south of the east entrance to Kyle Akin is deep, and foul with old moorings, but a narrow shelf on the northwest side has suitable depths for anchoring and it is sheltered from all but easterly winds. Noted as being full of fish cages and buoys.

Kyle Akin

A narrow passage, only 1½ cables wide at its west end, linking Loch Alsh with the Inner Sound, crossed by a bridge with 24m headroom.

Charts
2540 (1:20,000 and 1:12,500), 2209 (1:50,000)
OS map Landranger 33

Tides
Tidal streams in Kyle Akin vary widely between springs and neaps, and are affected by barometric pressure, wind direction, rain and melting snow.

At neaps, the wind in particular may reverse the direction of flow, a southerly or southwest wind tending towards a west-going stream, and a northerly wind tending towards an east-going stream.

To present the information as simply as possible, perhaps over-simplifying it:

The east-going stream begins –0300 Ullapool (+0050 Dover) at springs, and +0100 Ullapool (–0320 Dover) at neaps

The west-going stream begins +0330 Ullapool (–0050 Dover) at springs and –0600 Ullapool (+0110 Dover) at neaps.

The west-going stream is usually the stronger, running at up to 4kns at an extra spring tide.

For more detail see the *Admiralty Pilot*.

Constant –0030 Ullapool (–0450 Dover)

Height in metres

MHWS	MHWN	MTL	MLWN	MLWS
5·3	3·9	3·0	2·2	0·8

Dangers and marks
Eileanan Dubha, a group of islands at the east end of the kyle north of mid-channel, are marked by a white lattice light beacon 9m in height on their south side.

Off Rubha Ard Treisnis, the point of Skye south of Eileanan Dubha, a drying reef extends ½ cable northeastward.

String Rock which dries, 1½ cables off the south shore 1¾ cables southwest of Eileanan Dubha, is marked by a red can light buoy.

Drying rocks lie to the west of String Rock, up to 1½ cables from the shore.

North of Eileanan Dubha at Kyle of Lochalsh several jetties and piers project from the shore but the clear passage north of the islands is a cable wide. Rocks drying and submerged lie up to ¾ cable from the north shore west of Kyle of Lochalsh.

Kyle Akin lighthouse at the west end of the passage is entirely dwarfed by the bridge and no longer lit.

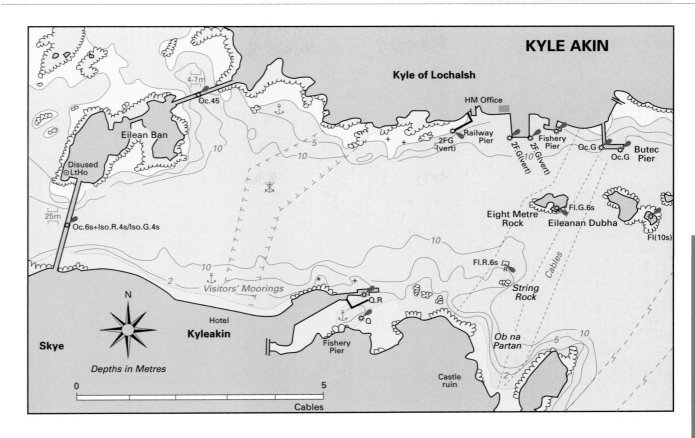

Black Eye Rock red can light buoy, two cables north of the head of a jetty at a quarry on Skye, west of the west entrance to the kyle, marks the most northeasterly of a patch of submerged rocks.

Bogha Beag, a reef which dries 0·6m lies three cables west-southwest of the light buoy. Another red can light buoy lies 3½ cables west of Black Eye Rock light buoy.

Fork Rocks green conical light buoy ¼ mile northwest of the lighthouse marks submerged rocks on the east side of the passage, and Carrach green conical light buoy, with a racon, lies seven cables northwest of the lighthouse.

Lights
Eileanan Dubha light beacon Fl(2)10s9m5M
Eight Metre Rock Fl.G.6s5m5M
String Rock light buoy Fl.R.6s
BUTEC Jetty Oc.G.6s at each end of its head
Kyleakin Ferry Slipway Q.R
Dolphin Q
Lights at bridge
Oc.6s at mid-span, Iso.R.4s to SSW, Iso.G.4s to north-northeast, Q.Y at either side of fairway.
Blackeye Rock light buoy Fl.R.6s
Bow Rock light buoy Fl(2)R.12s
Quarry jetty 2F.R(vert)
Fork Rocks light buoy Fl.G.6s
Carrach light buoy Fl(2)G.12s

String Rock buoy with Skye Bridge beyond. The buoy must be passed on its north side

Kyleakin harbour with pontoons. The pontoons at Kyle of Lochalsh are immediately above the tallest mast in the foreground, the hotel to the left, the harbour office to the right, and the Railway Pier with fuel berth to the right again

At night
The succession of lateral buoys make the passage relatively straightforward. Note that the Q.R light at Kyleakin slipway is not visible from either entrance to the kyle.

Anchorages
Kyleakin, 57°16′·4N 5°43′·5W; a small pool on the south side of Kyle Akin entered through a dredged channel between the ferry slip and a half-tide rock one cable east of it. Most of the inner part of the inlet dries, as well as the bay on its southeast side.

A fishery pier with two dolphins stands on the south side of the pool and a pontoon for small craft lies in the middle of the pool.

A yacht should be able to moor alongside the pontoon, although it may be necessary to raft up. Pay at Kyle harbour office.

Supplies
Shops, Post Office, telephone, hotel, showers and laundry at youth hostel, garage (one mile). Bus to Kyle of Lochalsh every half hour.

Visitors' moorings are laid north of Kyleakin, off the King's Arms Hotel; do not anchor to the east of the hotel as cables cross the kyle there. Disturbed by passing traffic, and swell in northerly wind. The bottom is blue clay.

Ob na Partan, south of String Rock buoy (not named on chart), has cables running from the head of the bay to the mainland, but ½ cable from the west side there is a depth of 7m clear of the cables.

Kyle of Lochalsh
57°16′·8N 5°42′·7W

Berth at pontoon west of the Railway Pier.

Note drying reef to west of pontoon, especially if making for north face of pontoon. Water at pontoon. Pay at harbour office.

Supplies
Shops (including butcher, baker, hardware, Post Office, bank, telephone, garage, gas (not *Calor Gas*), hotel. *Calor Gas* delivered from Balmacara ℡ 01599 566226 for a small charge. Seafood restaurant at railway station. Diesel at Railway Pier (see harbour office at new lifeboat house west of pier, or call *Kyle Harbour* on Ch 11).

Kyleakin from west with visitors' moorings in the foreground *Tim Whittome*

Tourist information office, showers at car park (up steps from old ferry slip). Doctor, dentist, chemist. General marine and electronic repairs. Swimming Pool. Bus to Kyleakin every half hour. Bus to Edinburgh/Glasgow and train to Inverness and south.

Kyle Harbour ☎ 01599 534167.

Anchorage

The bay ½ mile west of Railway Pier is clear north of the cable area, with moderate depth for anchoring on sand with patches of weed.

Kyle of Lochalsh *Tim Whittome*

V. The Inner Sound

The Inner Sound, which extends some 20 miles from Broadford Bay to the north end of Rona, together with the Sound of Raasay (*see Chapter VI*) and Loch Carron, provide an area of sheltered water with spectacular scenery and a wide variety of anchorages; Lochs Torridon and Gairloch may be reached without rounding a major headland.

Cloud caps blowing off the Skye hills are taken to be an indication of imminent squalls.

The sound is described in the following sequence: Loch Carron to Loch Torridon and Loch Gairloch. Broadford and Caolas Scalpay, Portree and the Sound of Raasay, Rona and north and northeast Skye are described in *Chapter VI*.

Charts

2209, 2210 (1:50,000)
OS Explorer map 428

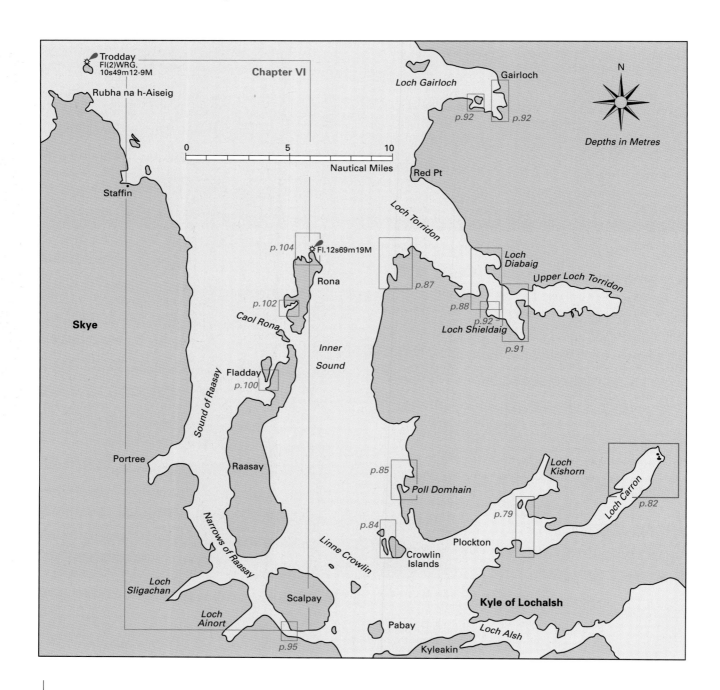

Loch Carron (outer part) and Loch Kishorn

57°21'N 5°42'W

Charts

2498 (1:25,000), 2528 (1:15,000)
OS Landranger map 24

Tides

Tidal streams are negligible.
Constant –0010 Ullapool (–0430 Dover)
Height in metres

MHWS	MHWN	MTL	MLWN	MLWS
5·1	3·8	2·9	2·0	0·7

The northwest side of the loch is clean and steep-to, but the southeast side is indented with many bays (some of which are suitable for occasional anchorage), with off-lying islands and drying rocks.

A course from Carrach Rock green light buoy, seven cables north-northwest of Skye Bridge, towards An Dubh-aird, a promontory four miles northeast, keeping two cables off each island and point passes clear of all hidden dangers, although a drying reef southwest of Black Islands, ¾ mile north-northeast of the light buoy, lies close to this line.

For the inner part of Loch Carron *see page 82*.

Minor anchorages

Camas an t-Strathaidh, 57°20'N 5°41'W, ¾ mile south of An Dubh-aird can be entered by either side of Eilean Dubh Dhurinish, the most northwesterly island in the entrance.

A drying reef extends more than a cable southwest, and a submerged reef up to a cable east-southeast, of the island.

The sides and head of the bay are shoal and drying, with drying rocks more than a cable from the shore.

Kishorn Island, 57°22'·5N 5°39'W; the anchorage is between the island and Rubha na h-Airde, the promontory on the south side of Loch Kishorn.

Drying rocks extend more than a cable south-southwest of the island, leaving a passage less than a cable wide between Kishorn Island and Garbh Eilean (Garra Islands).

If approaching from seaward, make for the middle of Garbh Eilean and keep less than ½ cable from that island; the approach by the north side of the island is safer.

Head of Loch Kishorn A reef drying 3·6m lies four cables from the east shore northwest of Achintraid village, and most of the area between the reef and the shore dries.

Anchor between the reef and a promontory three cables south of it.

Alternatively, west of Ardarroch on the north side of the head of the loch, off boat houses northeast of an islet on the east side of the mouth of River Kishorn.

Shop, Post Office, garage (petrol and diesel) on main road about ¼ mile from Ardarroch.

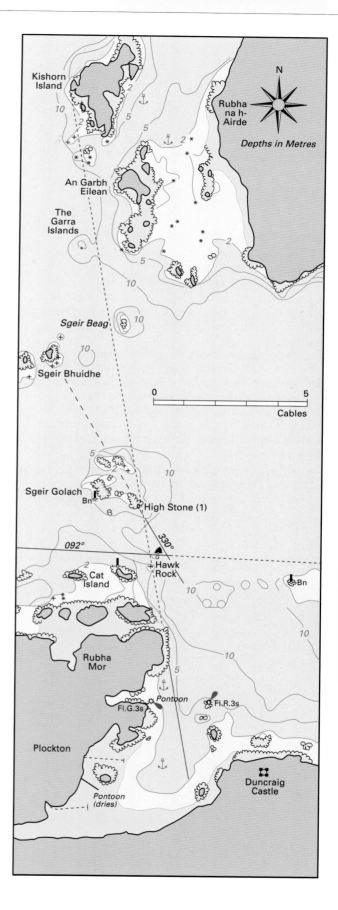

V. THE INNER SOUND

Plockton

57°20'·5N 5°38'·5W

Charts
2528 (1:15,000)
OS maps *24, 25*

Tides
Tidal streams are negligible.
Constant –0020 Ullapool (–0440 Dover)
Height in metres

MHWS	MHWN	MTL	MLWN	MLWS
5·5	4·1	3·1	2·2	0·8

Dangers and marks
Dangers and marks in the approach to Plockton are described below; those for the passage further up Loch Carron are described in later pages.

Cat Island (Eilean a' Chait) is a tidal islet north of Rubha Mor, the promontory north of Plockton, on which stands a conspicuous white disused lighthouse.

Drying rocks extend more than a cable northwest of rocks and islets standing above water between An Dubh-aird 1¼ miles west-southwest, and Cat Island.

The south tangent of Eilean an t-Sratha, the largest of Strome Islands (or alternatively the summit of Creag Mhaol, east of Strome Islands) open north of Cat Island 092° leads clear of the most northerly of these drying rocks.

Sgeir Golach, an area of drying rocks about ¼ mile across, lies ¼ mile north of Cat Island.

High Stone, the southeast point of these rocks is 1m high, and an iron tripod beacon with a basket topmark stands on the southwest point.

A drying rock lies nearly ½ cable south of the line between the beacon and High Stone.

Sgeir Bhuidhe, 4m high, and Sgeir a' Chinn 1m high, lie about ¾ mile north of Cat Island.

Sgeir Beag, ¼ mile east-northeast of Sgeir Bhuidhe, dries 1·5m and is very dangerous if passing direct between Loch Kishorn and Plockton.

Hawk Rock, almost awash at LW lies ¾ cable east-northeast of Cat Island. High Stone in line with Sgeir Bhuidhe 330° leads east of Hawk Rock.

Alternatively, a conspicuous waterfall on the north shore of Loch Kishorn in line with Sgeir Golach beacon bearing 325° leads close west of Hawk Rock.

A very small green conical buoy has been laid just northeast of Hawk Rock.

Duncraig Castle, about ¾ mile south-southeast of Cat Island, is conspicuous.

Bogha Dubh Sgeir, on which is a beacon similar to that on Sgeir Golach, lies ½ mile east of Cat Island.

Plockton Rocks drying at half tide, marked by a metal column with a red rectangular topmark, lie north-northwest of Sgeir Bhuidhe, an islet (different from the one of the same name above) off the southeast shore. High Stone, or the west side of Kishorn Island in line with the east tangent of Rubha Mor leads west of these rocks.

A drying reef lies nearly ½ cable off Roinn an Fhaing at Plockton village.

Lights
At head of new pontoon Fl.G.3s
Plockton Rocks Fl.R.3s

Plockton from north with Cat Island in the foreground *Tim Whittome*

Plockton from west with pontoons for dinghies to the right of the small island in the foreground. Note Plockton Rocks at the left *Tim Whittome*

Sgeir Buidhe, Plockton

Plockton from south

Directions

After passing An Dubh-aird, steer about 060° until Eilean an t-Sratha is clear open north of Cat Island; steer to pass between Cat Island and High Stone until High Stone is in line with Sgeir Bhuidhe, 330°. Steer to keep this line astern (or use the alternative transit above) until Rubha Mor is abeam and steer for Plockton village.

Anchorage

Anchor off the slip at the north end of the village if space can be found clear of moorings (as well as

thick weed), or between the village and Duncraig Castle, clear of Plockton Rocks and Sailing Club starting line, indicated by a flag pole on shore and a large yellow spherical buoy in transit.

Visitors' moorings in southeast part of bay; no pick-ups. Pay at shop or hotels.

A pontoon has been established (for short-term use only) at the stone slipway at the north end of the village. Pay at shop or hotels.

Supplies

Shop, hotels, telephones, *Calor Gas* from shop. Water from tap (hidden in an old pump inside a small fence on the village green), or from a tap at rear of toilets at car park; use of a hose may also be offered from house by the slip at the north end of the village. Showers at Plockton Hotel. Laundry ask at Leisure Marine. Diesel from Calum Mackenzie (Leisure Marine ☎ 01599 544306). Sailing club.

Strome Narrows and Inner Loch Carron

Charts

2528 (1:15,000) only as far east as Strome Narrows; for the inner loch use *2209*
OS maps Landranger 24, 25

Tides

In Strome Narrows tidal streams run at up to 3kns but are negligible elsewhere.
The in-going stream begins +0605 Ullapool (+0145 Dover)
The out-going stream begins +0005 Ullapool (−0415 Dover)

Constant −0010 Ullapool (−0430 Dover)
Height in metres

MHWS	MHWN	MTL	MLWN	MLWS
5·1	3·8	2·9	2·0	0·7

Dangers and marks

Bo Dubh Sgeir, ½ mile east of Cat Island, is marked by a beacon similar to that at Sgeir Golach.

Ulluva, two cables off the south shore, seven cables southeast of Bo Dubh Sgeir, is marked by a stone cairn faded yellow in colour, and surrounded by drying rocks.

The bay to starboard dries off two cables and, at the narrows, a shoal area lies on the south side.

Directions

From the approach to Plockton, pass south of Bo Dubh Sgeir beacon, and two cables north of Ulluva island.

Lochcarron

⊕ On leading line 328° 57°23'·5N 5°28'·6W

An extensive village on the northwest shore of the loch.

Slumbay Island, a peninsula at the south end of the village, partly shelters a bay known as Slumbay Harbour the shores of which dry off more than a cable. Slumbay Harbour is now full of moorings and a visiting yacht is unlikely to find space to anchor inside, although anchoring off the mouth is possible.

Sgeir Chreagach and Sgeir Fhada stand ½ mile offshore on drying reefs.

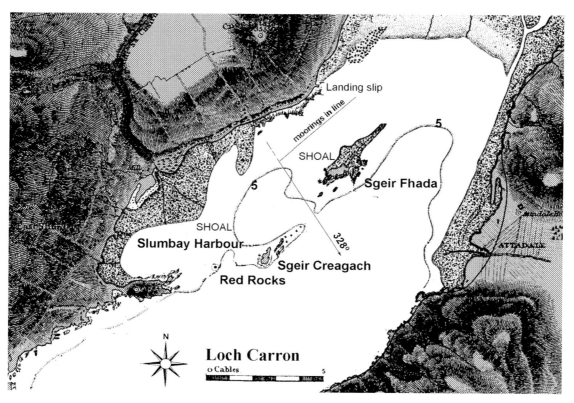

Loch Carron

Shed with green doors

Lochcarron: the shed with green doors above the village, in line with a fence running up the hillside into a plantation bearing 328°, leads between Sgeir Creagach and Sgeir Fhada *Rob Teago*

Red Rocks, some of which are submerged and some awash at LWS, lie between Slumbay Island and Sgeir Chreagach.

The foreshore in front of the village dries off in places up to ¼ mile; there is a drying area ¼ mile northeast of Sgeir Fhada, and the head of the loch dries off for one mile.

The approach between Sgeir Chreagach and Sgeir Fhada is identified by the following line: a pale green shed with two dark green doors, bearing 328°, in line with a fence running up the hillside to the middle of a line of fir trees (*see photo*).

A jetty/slipway stands in front of the hotel north of Sgeir Fhada. Visitors' moorings (yellow, marked *visitor*) are laid in 3m off the jetty.

Approach

Leave Sgeir Creagach a cable to port, and turn onto the leading line 328° described above. When clear of the shoal water north of Sgeir Fhada, turn towards the moorings (these have been laid in line indicating the line on which to approach).

Payment is collected on behalf of Lochcarron Pier Trust. The risers are stated to have been renewed in 2010.

Supplies

Shops, Post Office, telephone, hotel, bank, medical centre.

Petrol, diesel and water at garage at head of jetty. *Calor Gas* at West End Garage. Bicycle hire.

Railway station four miles.

Slipping for dinghies and 'moderate sized' trailer sailers.

Drying out is possible alongside the old ferry slip at North Strome.

Caolas Mor

⊕ 57°21′N 5°50′W

Charts

2480, 2498 (1:25,000)
OS Explorer map 428

Dangers and marks

In the passage northeast of Crowlin Islands, rocks submerged and drying on the northeast side of the passage extend 3½ cables south of Aird Mhor on the west side of Loch Toscaig. The northeast tangent of Eilean na Ba open of a 5m rock off the southwest side of Aird Mhor, 334°, leads close southwest of the outermost rock.

A rock which dries 1·1m lies two cables north of Eilean Beag, the most northwesterly of the Crowlin Islands, with other rocks between the drying rock and the island.

Fish cages east of the north end of Crowlin Beag are marked by a yellow can light buoy.

Lights

A light beacon, Fl.6s32m6M, stands on the west side of Eilean Beag
Y can light buoy Fl.Y

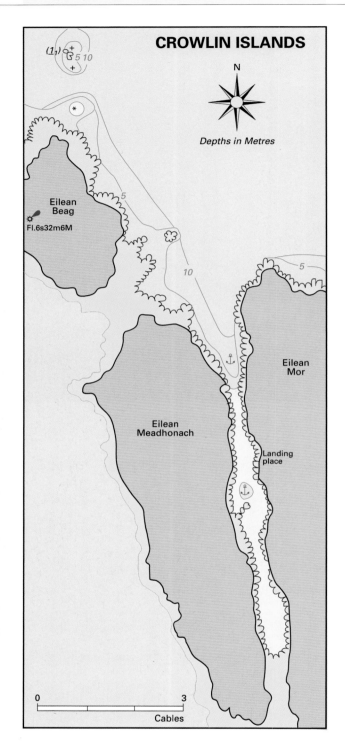

CROWLIN ISLANDS

N

Depths in Metres

Eilean
Beag
Fl.6s32m6M

5

10

5

Eilean
Mor

Eilean
Meadhonach

Landing
place

0   3
Cables

Crowlin Harbour; MFV *Barcadale* is anchored where the
Admiralty chart shows the deepest water, although the
deepest part is just north of the end of the drying reef
Norman Smith

In approach note the rocks described above;
coming from west there is a clear passage two cables
wide north of Bo Du, the most northerly rock,
which dries 1·5m.

Shellfish-farming equipment on both sides of the
loch is marked by orange buoys.

Camas na Ba on the west side of the loch is
occupied by moorings.

Crowlin Harbour, 57°21′N 5°50′·6W, between Eilean
Mor and Eilean Meadhonach, provides an
occasional anchorage in its entrance.

Above half tide, the creek can be entered but most
of it is shallow and the flood tide runs strongly in
the entrance.

Approaching from the west, keep at least ¼ mile
north of Eilean Beag to avoid the drying rock
described above.

Poll Domhain and Poll Creadha

57°24′N 5°49′W

Charts

2480 (1:25,000)
OS Landranger map 24

Tides

Constant −0015 Ullapool (−0435 Dover)
Height in metres

MHWS	MHWN	MTL	MLWN	MLWS
5·3	4·0	3·1	2·2	0·7

Poll Domhain

Poll Domhain is entered by the north side of Ard
Ban which is identified by a conspicuous white
beach on its west side.

Tides

In Caolas Mor tidal streams run at 1kn at springs.
The southeast-going stream begins +0605 Ullapool
(+0145 Dover)
The northwest-going stream begins +0005 Ullapool
(−0415 Dover)

Anchorages

Loch Toscaig, 57°22′N 5°48′·5W. Occasional anchorage
east or southeast of the pier.

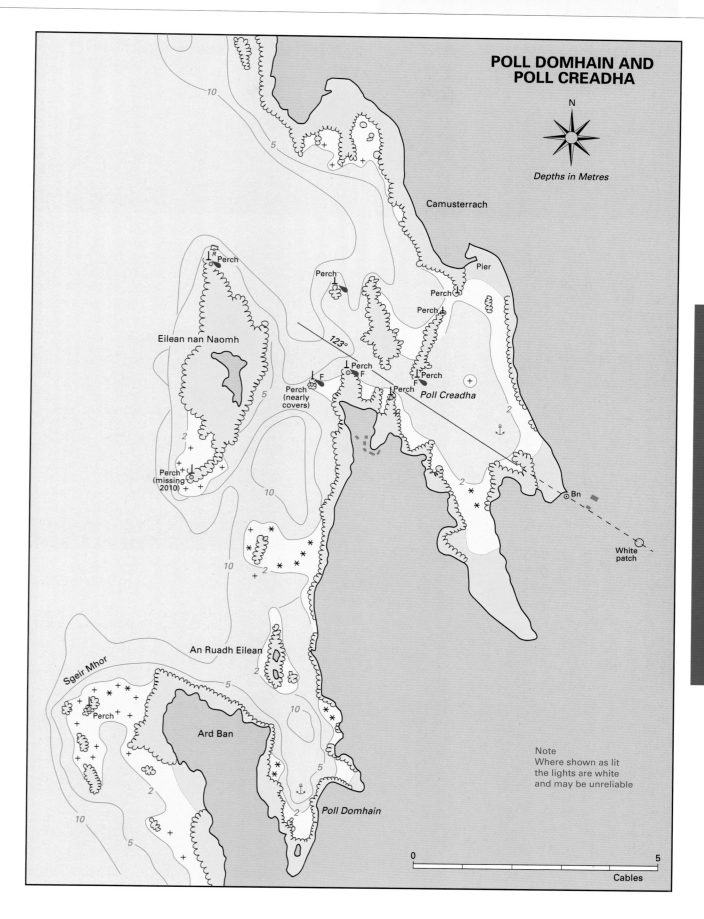

POLL DOMHAIN AND
POLL CREADHA

N

Depths in Metres

Camusterrach

Pier

R Perch

Perch

Perch

Perch

123°

Perch

Perch
F

F Perch

Perch
(nearly
covers)

Perch

F Perch

Poll Creadha

Eilean nan Naomh

2

Perch
(missing
2010)

10

10

2

Bn

White
patch

10

2

Sgeir Mhor

An Ruadh Eilean

2

10

Perch

Ard Ban

5

5

2

Note
Where shown as lit
the lights are white
and may be unreliable

10

5

2

Poll Domhain

0   5

Cables

V. THE INNER SOUND

Poll Domhain

Poll Creadha from north; Camusterrach pier at bottom of photo

Sgeir Mhor, which dries 3·2m two cables west of Ard Ban, is marked by a thin steel perch which is almost covered at HW. The high water line of the east side of Eilean na Ba in line with the east side of Eilean Mor (Crowlin Islands), 168°, leads west of Sgeir Mhor.

Drying reefs extend a cable north of Ard Ban. From northwest, pass south of An Ruadh Eilean. The head of the pool is narrowed by drying reefs on either side.

Extensive reefs lie on the west side of the inlet. The best landing place is on the west side of the more southerly reef.

Poll Creadha

Poll Creadha is obstructed by drying reefs, and safe access depends on the perches shown on the plan being in place. It should not be attempted if any swell is running.

The perches have been lit in the past with fixed W lights, but these are to be upgraded to international standards.

Supplies

None. Post office, shop and hotel at Applecross, four miles.

Poll Creadha from southeast; slipway on west shore

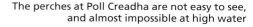

The perches at Poll Creadha are not easy to see, and almost impossible at high water

Perch

Inner Sound

The direction of buoyage throughout the Inner Sound and Sound of Raasay is northwards although the flood tide runs southwards.

Charts

2209, 2210 (1:50,000)
OS map *24*

Tides

In the Inner Sound the flood stream runs south, and spring rates are no more than 1kn off headlands.
The south-going stream begins +0605 Ullapool (+0145 Dover)
The north-going stream begins –0005 Ullapool (–0415 Dover)

Dangers and marks

The fairway of Inner Sound is clean, but both in Caolas Mor, northeast of Crowlin Islands (above, page 83), and on a passage to Caol Mor between Scalpay and Raasay (below, page 96), there are specific dangers.

The Crowlin Islands, and Dun Caan on Raasay, the conspicuous plug of a former volcano, are useful reference marks.

Drying rocks lie up to two cables from the shore between ¾ and one mile south of the Range Control building (*see below*).

Underwater weapons testing is carried out in a restricted area between Raasay and the mainland marked by yellow pillar light buoys. Operations are controlled from the Range Control building at Ru na Lachan on the east shore seven miles north of Crowlin Beag. The buoys are as follows:

C in mid-sound 3½ miles northwest of Crowlin Beag.
D 5 cables off Raasay, 2¾ miles west of C.
B about one mile north-northwest of the Range Control building.

Four special yellow buoys near the Range Control building mark a cable area.

When underwater testing is being carried out a red flag is shown at the Range Control building (or, by night, a red light). A vessel approaching the restricted area will be contacted by VHF or by a patrol boat, usually a naval MFV. It is helpful for yachts approaching this area to call Range Control on VHF and to listen to traffic on Ch 13. Yachts will be directed to pass clear of the restricted area to one side, usually to the west. Information about each day's testing programme is broadcast on Ch 08 at 0800 and 1800.

Lights

Crowlin Islands light beacon Fl.6s32m6M
Eyre Point, Caol Mor Fl.WR.3s5m9/6M
Ru na Lachan Oc.WR.8s21m10M
Restricted area buoys:
C Fl.Y.5s
D Fl.Y.10s
B Fl.Y.10s
Cable area buoys off Range Control building Fl.Y.5s

Garbh Eilean (south end of Rona) Fl.3s
Various other light beacons on the east side of Rona have no navigational significance.
Rona lighthouse Fl.12s69m19M is obscured from 358°-050°

Ob Chuaig

57°26'·5N 06°01'·4W

An occasional anchorage south of the entrance to Loch Torridon, with a sandy beach at the head and several rocks in the bay (*see plan*).

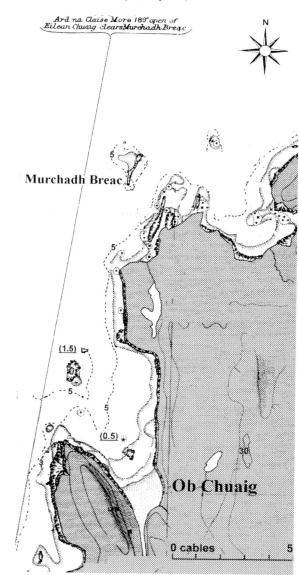

Ob Chuaig, an occasional anchorage at the mouth of Loch Torridon *Anna Lawrence*

Loch Torridon

57°35'N 5°45'W

An impressive loch in three parts, joined by passages four and two cables wide, surrounded by spectacular mountains in its upper part.

Charts

2210 (1:50,000), obsolete chart 2638 (1:25,000) with depths in fathoms

OS Explorer maps 428 for southwest side of Loch Torridon, *433* for rest of the Loch; *OS Landranger map 24*

Tides

The in-going stream begins –0605 Ullapool (+0200 Dover)

The out-going stream begins –0005 Ullapool (–0425 Dover)

Constant –0020 Ullapool (–0440 Dover)

Height in metres

MHWS	MHWN	MTL	MLWN	MLWS
5·6	4·2	3·2	2·2	0·7

Dangers and marks in the outer loch

The entrance is three miles wide between Rubha na Fearn on the south side and Red Point on the north.

Murchadh Breac, three cables offshore, a mile west of Rubha na Fearn dries 1·5m and is a danger to yachts coming from south.

Murchadh Breac is cleared on its west side by keeping Ard na Claise Moire, a point five miles south, open west of Eilean Chuaig 187°.

The school house at Diabaig in Loch Torridon (the most southerly house there), open of Rubha na Fearn 098°, leads north of Murchadh Breac.

Sgeir a' Ghair, 1¼ cables northeast of Rubha na Fearn, is 0·5m high.

Sgeir na Trian, 2m high, lies 1¼ miles south-southeast of Red Point, towards the north side of the entrance and is in the way when coming from, or heading, north.

Sgeir Ghlas, 1m high, lies outside the mouth of a bay, three cables offshore four cables east-southeast of Red Point.

The southwest shore between Rubha na Fearn and Ardheslaig, the promontory on the south side of the first narrows, is very broken with bays between rocky points and rocks which dry more than a cable from the shore.

The northeast shore is almost featureless as far as Rubha na h-Airde on the north side of the narrows.

Sgeir Dughall, 6m high, lies ¼ mile offshore seven cables northwest of Rubha na h-Airde.

Ard na Claise More *open of* Eilean Chuaig *clears* Murchadh Breac
View (*at Lat. 57° 35'5 N., Long. 5° 50'5 W., approx.*)

Minor anchorages in the outer loch

Camas Eilean, 1¼ miles west of Ardheslaig.

Occasional anchorage on the west or south side of the bay south of Eilean Mor. A fish cage is moored southeast of Eilean Mor; and the passage between Eilean Mor and the mainland is constricted by drying reefs.

Loch a' Chracaich, 57°33'N 5°44'W, a mile southwest of Ardheslaig.

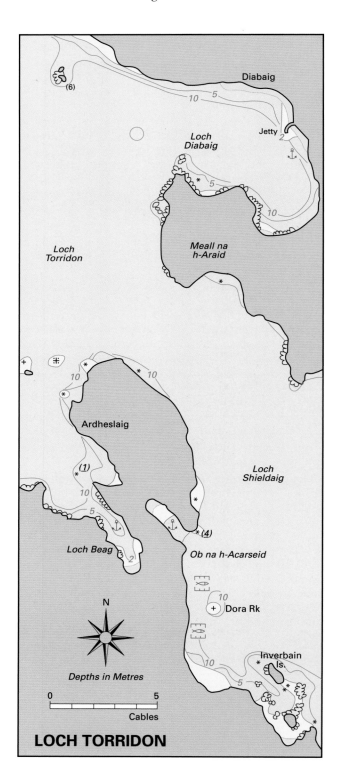

LOCH TORRIDON

Rocks drying 3m lie ½ cable east of Sgeir Glas off the north point of the bay, and submerged rocks lie about a cable from the south shore east of the mouth of a burn.

Fish cages are moored south of the north point and on the southeast side of the bay.

Anchor in the northwest corner, or at the south end of the southwest side of the bay; weed may be a problem. Telephone. No stores.

Loch Beag, 57°33′N 5°43′W, a narrow inlet ¾ mile south of Ardheslaig is occupied by fishing-boat moorings.

Dubh Sgeir, 2m high, lies ¼ mile west of Ardheslaig, northwest of the approach to the inlet.

A drying reef lies 1¼ cables east-northeast of Dubh Sgeir, and a submerged rock ½ cable north-northwest.

Other drying rocks lie near the shore further east.

A rock one cable northwest of the north point of Loch Beag dries 1m.

Rocks drying and submerged extend ¼ cable from either shore in places.

Several inshore fishing boats are moored in Loch Beag, but it is a useful alternative anchorage to Ob na h-Acairseid in easterly winds.

Red Bay, 57°38′N 5°48′W, immediately east of Red Point, gives good shelter from northerly winds off a sandy beach.

Sgeir Ghlas, 1m high, lies three cables south of the middle of the head of the bay, and a submerged rock lies ½ cable west of it. Salmon nets and fishing floats lie in the bay.

Telephone 1½ miles along track.

Loch Diabaig, 57°34′·5N 5°42′W, lies on the northeast side of the outer loch, northeast of Rubha na h-Airde.

Sgeir Dughall, 6m high, stands two cables offshore ¾ mile northwest of Rubha na h-Airde.

The bay on the south side of the head of the loch is full of fish cages.

Loch Beag, Loch Torridon *Anna Lawence*

Anchor either side of the jetty, the head of which stands on a reef which covers at high water.

Ob na h-Acarseid, 57°32′·5N 5°42′W, an inlet on the east side of Ardheslaig, is clean but very narrow.

Clach na Be off the north point of the entrance dries 4m.

Many fish cages are anchored off the east side of Ardheslaig, and a floating pipeline lying along the northwest side of the inlet supplies feed to the fish cages. Two Y light buoys mark the east limit of the fish farm, but there is one visitor's mooring in the inlet and some space to anchor. When approaching from the northwest leave both yellow flashing lights to starboard and pass inside the cages to access the mooring or anchor in the Ob. Look out for Dora Rock, covered at LW, close to the south yellow buoy.

Inverbain Islands, one mile west of Shieldaig Island, have a shallow basin on their south side which provides shelter for shoal draft boats or others at neaps.

Inverbain Islands showing the shallow pool south of Eilean Dughaill *John Shepherd*

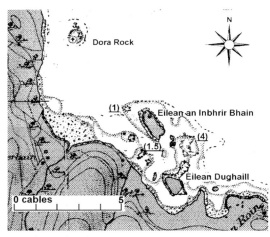

Inverbain Islands

A rock which dries 1·2m lies ½ cable west of Eilean an Inbhir Bhan, and drying rocks lie in the middle of the passage south of that island but an apparently clear channel lies between the rocks and the island.

A sheltered anchorage lies between Eilean Dughaill and the mainland. there are two approaches. A channel from the northwest between the tidal islets and the mainland. At a distance of about 25m from the mainland coast the minimum depth is about 1m MLWS where there is a small spit and a stream enters the sea.

A second approach is south of Eilean Dughaill; where indistinct leading marks lead across a rocky sill. One is just above the beach at the left end of a small area of beach cleared of boulders and weed) the second mark is in trees and is not visible south of the leading line. The bottom is mud, a yacht permanently moored there takes the ground at spring tides. A small pontoon with lobster gear is also moored there and has a line ashore to the island.

Loch Shieldaig

57°32′N 5°40′W

This is the middle part of Loch Torridon, with a good anchorage between Shieldaig Island, which is 41m high and thickly wooded and Shieldaig village on the east side of the loch.

Drying rocks extend a cable from the northwest point of the island and ½ cable north from its northeast side.

A rock ½ cable south of the point below the church at the north end of the village dries 2m.

The south end of the passage is blocked by drying and above-water rocks.

Supplies

Shops, Post Office, telephone, hotel. *Calor Gas* at Camas Doire Aonar on the west side of Loch Shieldaig.

Loch Torridon looking east over Ardheslaig peninsula to Loch Shieldaig

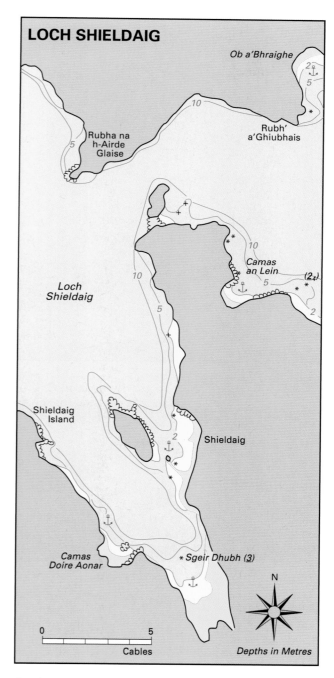

LOCH SHIELDAIG

Ob a'Bhraighe

Rubh' a'Ghiubhais

Rubha na h-Airde Glaise

Camas an Lein

Loch Shieldaig

Shieldaig Island

Shieldaig

Camas Doire Aonar

Sgeir Dhubh (3)

N

0   5
Cables   Depths in Metres

Upper Loch Torridon

A clean passage two cables wide leads from the northeast side of Loch Shieldaig to Upper Loch Torridon which is generally free from dangers apart from detached drying rocks in two places 1¼ cables off the south shore.

Occasional anchorages may be found in most of the inlets around the shore, depending on wind direction, but some are occupied by fish cages.

The upper loch is very squally if there is any wind.

Anchorages

Camas an Lein, on the east side of the peninsula which separates Loch Shieldaig from the upper loch, provides good shelter in westerly winds.

A rock dries 2·4m one cable off the south point of the bay.

Ob a' Bhraighe on the north shore north-northeast of Rubh' a' Ghiubhais, ¾ mile east-northeast of the narrows, has a rock which dries 1·5m ½ cable off the west side of the entrance.

Ob Gorm Beag has three rows of floats across it with a gap at alternate ends of each row, and a mooring for a fishing boat at the head.

Ob Gorm Mor has only two rows of floats, and there is more space to anchor.

At the *head of the loch*, the best anchorage is on the south side close to the southwest shore, between a jetty at Eilean Chasgaig ¼ mile northwest of the hotel and Rubha an t-Salainn, a wooded rocky promontory three cables northwest of it. Hotel nearby.

Torridon village, on the north side of the head of the loch, has a shop and a Post Office.

Anchor in quiet weather northwest of the head of a promontory which extends from the east shore.

Loch Gairloch

Charts

2528 (1:15,000), 2210 (1:50,000)
OS Landranger map 19; OS Explorer map 433

Tides

Constant –0020 Ullapool (–0440 Dover)
Height in metres

MHWS	MHWN	MTL	MLWN	MLWS
5·2	4·0	3·0	1·8	0·6

Dangers and marks

The loch is clean except within the inlets of the south shore and between Eilean Horrisdale and Loch Shieldaig.

Glas Eilean, towards the head of the loch, has a light beacon at its centre.

Longa Island lies ½ mile from the north point of the entrance; in Caolas Beag, the channel between Longa and the mainland, the shore dries for two cables.

Anchorages

The principal anchorage is southeast of Shieldaig Island, clear of the rocks described above.

The head of Loch Shieldaig dries for two cables and Sgeir Dhubh, in the middle of the loch 3½ cables from its head, dries 3m. Holding is said to be poor.

Holding east of the north tip of the island is reported to be very poor.

Camas Doire Aonar on the southwest shore is full of small-boat moorings, but good shelter and holding are found off the entrance in a strong southwest wind.

V. THE INNER SOUND

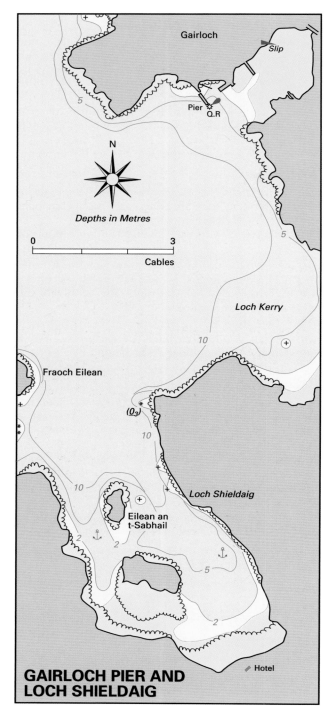

GAIRLOCH PIER AND LOCH SHIELDAIG

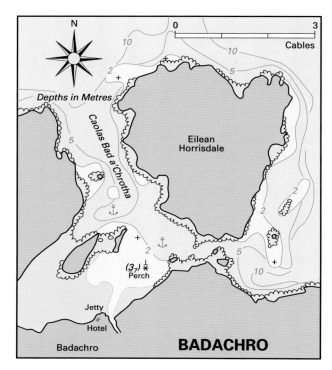

BADACHRO

Badachro, Gairloch, from the head of the slip

Lights

Glas Eilean Fl.WRG.6s9m6-4M
Gairloch Pier head Q.R.9m
Glas Eilean light beacon shows white towards the
  entrance clear of danger and towards Loch Shieldaig
  and the approach to Gairloch Pier.

Badachro (Caolas Bad a' Chrotha)

57°42'N 5°43'W

A well-sheltered inlet, easy to approach but quite
fully occupied by fishing boats and local yachts.

Dangers and marks

On the west side of the channel an above-water rock
stands at the east end of a drying reef leaving a
passage ½ cable wide between the rock and Eilean
Horrisdale; beware also of the drying reef to the east
of the visible rock.

A submerged rock lies ½ cable south-southeast of
the above-water rock at a depth of 0·9m.

A rock which dries 3·7m on the southeast side of
the fairway south of two tidal islets is marked by a
perch.

The head of the inlet dries off ¼ mile.

The fairway is lined with moorings on either side.

The hotel has two visitors' moorings.

A stone jetty and slipway stand on the west side of
the mouth of a river which runs out on the south
shore.

The bed of the river effectively dries and the
current is strong, especially after rain but, with care,
a yacht can go alongside after half flood to take on
water from a hose.

Loch Shieldaig, Gairloch

A post stands on the west side of the slip and, when the foot of the post is covered, there is 2·4m depth at the east side of the slip.

If Badachro is too crowded, space can be found to anchor in *The Bird's Nest*, south-southeast of Eilean Horrisdale, (*see below*) The passage south of Eilean Horrisdale, although tortuous, can be negotiated with care.

Supplies

Shop, telephone, hotel, baths at hotel, the hotel, water at slip, *Calor Gas*, chandlery, diesel from chandlery.

Other anchorages

The Bird's Nest, 57°41'·5N 5°41'W, or east of Horrisdale Island, inshore of Sgeir Dubh Bheag.

Loch Shieldaig, 57°41'·5N 5°41'W, in the southeast corner of Loch Gairloch, is occupied by moorings, many of them belonging to east coast fishing boats and often not used during the summer.

If there is no space in the main part of the loch, anchor south-southwest of Eilean an t-Sabhail or in Camas na h-Airighe, southwest of Fraoch Eilean.

A rock which dries 0·3m lies ¼ cable off the east point of the entrance to Loch Shieldaig.

Submerged rocks lie up to ¾ cable southwest of Fraoch Eilean, and a rock one cable south of the island dries 1·1m.

Drying rocks lie less than a cable off the east side of Eilean Horrisdale but shelter may be found clear of them.

Consult harbourmaster before berthing, or mooring in Loch Shieldaig. VHF Ch 12
☎ 01445 712140, *Mobile* 07769 671966.

Loch Kerry is partly occupied by fish cages and a submerged rock lies in the middle of the bay one cable from the southwest shore.

Flowerdale Bay

Gairloch Pier, 57°42'·6N 5°41'W, is used by fishing boats, and dues are charged. A 60m pontoon has been installed, with a depth of 2m on the north side and 3m on the south side. Light 2FG(vert).

The river mouth dries off two cables and yachts should go no further in than a line joining the head of the east pier and the promontory on the south side of the river.

Landing at steps at old stone pier.

Supplies

Shop, Post Office, telephone, hotel, bank, petrol at garage, and diesel at pier. Water by hose at pier, *Calor Gas* and mechanical repairs – ask at garage. Launching slip, sailing club, chandlery.

Showers and meals at The Old Inn, east of the bridge over the river.

Gairloch Pier pontoon

VI. Sound of Raasay and approaches

Corry Pier, Broadford from south. The drying rock south of the pierhead is not showing

Broadford Pier. Corry Pier is on the far side of the bay

Charts

2498, 2534 (1:25,000), 2209 (1:50,000)
OS maps Landranger 24, 32; OS Explorer maps 412 for south side of Inner Sound, *409* for rest of Inner Sound.

Broadford Bay

Tides

In Caolas Pabay, the northeast-going stream begins +0550 Ullapool (+0130 Dover)
The southwest-going stream begins –0010 Ullapool (–0430 Dover) at a spring rate of 1 kn

Dangers and marks

The Skye shore is fringed with drying reefs and rocks, in places extending 3½ cables from the shore; the most extensive are south of Pabay.

Drying rocks extend ½ mile south-southwest of Pabay to Sgeir Ghobhlach on which stands an iron beacon 9m high with a cage topmark.

Submerged rocks lie 1½ cables southwest of the beacon.

Directions

From Kyle Akin pass north of both of the red buoys west of the Skye Bridge and from the second buoy (*Bow Rock*) steer for Sgeir Ghobhlach beacon; when the east side of Pabay is abeam steer for the southwest corner of Broadford Bay.

Anchorages

In Broadford Bay a convenient anchorage is off Corry Pier on the west side of the bay but a drying rock lies about ½ cable south of the head of the pier.

It may be possible to lie at the south side of the pier to go ashore for stores, but all space may be taken by fishing boats and some crew should stay aboard in case it is necessary to move.

It may be possible to lie at the drying pier on the south side of the bay near high water.

Supplies at Broadford

Shops, Post Office, telephone, hotel, petrol and diesel at garage. Launderette at Broadford Hotel. 24-hour fuel, *Calor Gas*, shopping and launderette at Sutherland's garage. Dentist and hospital.

Caolas Scalpay

Tides

The east-going stream begins +0550 Ullapool (+0130 Dover)

The west-going stream begins –0010 Ullapool (–0430 Dover), at a spring rate of 1kn

Directions

From Kyle Akin, approach as for Broadford and continue on that course until ¼ mile beyond a point where the beacon is abeam.

Alternatively, pass north of Pabay, but note that drying reefs extend three cables north and northwest of the island.

In Caolas Scalpay, drying reefs extend one cable from Scalpay and a shingle bank extends north from Skye, with a depth of only 0·1m in the narrowest part between them.

A leading line to help in finding the channel is the school house at Dunan, a white building on the Skye shore, west of the narrows, under the peak of An Coileach which is beyond, and to the right of, the summit of Am Meall, 291°.

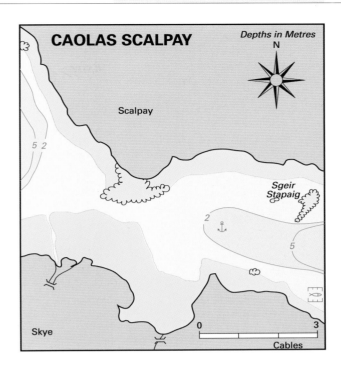

Caolas Scalpay with the shallow rocky channel showing clearly under water

VI. SOUND OF RAASAY AND APPROACHES

Anchorage

As convenient either east or west of the narrows. Either may be squally.

Note Sgeir Stapaig which dries, a cable off the Scalpay shore east of the narrows.

Fish cages are moored off both shores, those to the south marked by light buoys, Q.Y.

Skye Boat Centre, on the south shore, west of the narrows, has moorings, slip, floating jetty, Dive service, and can provide mechanical and electronic repairs. ☎ 01471 822070.

Loch Ainort

57°17′N 6°02′W

A wild and rather featureless loch surrounded by high hills.

Anchor either at Luib on the southeast side of the loch, in a slight indentation off the mouth of a valley, or in the south or west corners of the head of the loch.

Caol Mor and Sound of Raasay

57°20′N 6°05′W

Charts

2534, 2498 (1:25,000) for approach, *2209* (1:50,000) OS *Landranger map 24*

Tides

In Caol Mor, the spring rate is 1kn; in Linne Crowlin, southwest of Crowlin Islands it is ½kn, and, between Scalpay and Longay, 2kns.

The southeast and east-going stream begins +0605 Ullapool (+0145 Dover)

The northwest and west-going stream begins +0005 Ullapool (−0415 Dover)

Constant −0025 Ullapool (−0445 Dover)

Height in metres

MHWS	MHWN	MTL	MLWN	MLWS
5·3	3·7	2·9	1·9	0·7

Dangers and marks in the approach to Caol Mor from southeast

Longay, east-northeast of Scalpay, has drying reefs ¾ cable southwest and 1½ cables northwest of it.

Sgeir Dhearg, an islet 8m high surrounded by reefs lies ¾ mile northwest of Scalpay.

Gulnare Rock which dries, halfway between Sgeir Dhearg and Scalpay, is marked on its south side by a red can light buoy.

Sgeir Thraid, a reef drying 4m six cables west-northwest of Sgeir Dhearg, is marked by a red iron beacon with a cage topmark.

Pass either southwest or northeast of these rocks as convenient with due care.

Lights

A light beacon Fl.WR.3s5m9/6M stands at Eyre Point on the northeast side of Caol Mor showing red over the dangers described above, and white elsewhere.
Gulnare Rock light buoy Fl.R.5s

Occasional anchorage

Hallaig an open bay on the east side of Raasay, two miles north of Eyre Point light beacon, exposed north – northeast, with a shingle beach at the head, and a shingle spit extending north from Rudha na Leac at the east side of the bay. An occasional anchorage with possibilities for exploring ashore.

Loch Sligachan

57°19′N 6°07′W

Like Loch Ainort, a wild and mountainous loch subject to squalls but convenient for an expedition to the Red Cuillins.

Tides

The spring rate in the entrance is 1½kns.
The in-going stream begins +0605 Ullapool (+0145 Dover)
The out-going stream begins −0015 Ullapool (−0435 Dover)

Dangers and marks

The entrance is partly blocked by An Corran, a drying spit on the north side. The end of the spit is reported to be marked by a small (unofficial?) unlit starboard-hand buoy. A ferry to Raasay operates from a slip on the south shore of the loch.

A shoal extends four cables from the south shore outside the entrance to Bo Sligachan which dries 0·2m.

Hallaig, Raasay

Loch Sligachan from southwest, with the spit An Corran at the left-hand side and shoals showing under water

Sconser Lodge, a stone house on the shore east of the entrance with a few trees around it, in line with the summit of Sgurr Mhairi, the highest hill on the south side of the loch, 215° leads west-northwest of the shoals to the entrance. One cable from the shore turn west and then west-northwest to pass south of An Corran which shows pale below the water.

Anchorages

Peinchorran, within the entrance on the north side.

Sgeir Dhubh 0·6m high lies a cable off the northeast side of the bay and disused underwater cables (marked by rusty red cable beacons) lie across the loch ½ cable further west from a ruined slip on the north shore.

Anchor to the west of the ruined slip.

The head of the loch dries for more than ½ mile and banks on either side dry for more than a cable in places.

Anchor towards the head of the loch, in a depth of not less than 5m as the bottom rises abruptly.

Sligachan Inn is famous as a climbers' hostelry.

Raasay Narrows

57°20'·5N 6°05'W

Tides

The south-going stream begins –0605 Ullapool (+0200 Dover)

The north-going stream begins –0040 Ullapool (–0500 Dover)

Constant –0025 Ullapool (–0445 Dover)

Height in metres

MHWS	MHWN	MTL	MLWN	MLWS
5·3	3·7	2·9	1·9	0·7

Dangers and marks

(In sequence from south to north)

The passage is ½ mile wide between An Aird on Skye and Eilean Aird nan Gobhar, southwest of Ardhuish on Raasay, northeast of An Aird.

Suisnish Pier (disused) stands at the southwest point of Raasay.

Rainy Rocks, drying 1·1m, lie one cable east of the east point of An Aird.

Penfold Rock red can light buoy two cables northeast of An Aird, and Jackal Rock green conical light buoy six cables east of An Aird, both mark rocks at a depth of 2·9m.

McMillan's Rock, four cables north of An Aird at a depth of 0·4m, is marked on its west side by a green conical light buoy.

Raasay Narrows. Camas a'Mhor-bheoil is at the left and Balmeanach Bay at the right

A submerged rock lies a cable west of Eilean Aird nan Gobhar at a depth of 1·3m.

Sgeir Chnapach, 3m high, lies 1¼ miles north of Ardhuish, three cables from Raasay, with drying rocks inshore of it.

Direction

Pass northeast of Penfold Rock light buoy to keep clear of Rainy Rocks.

McMillan's Rock light buoy should be passed on its west side, or not less than a cable to the east.

Lights

Eyre Point light beacon Fl.WR.3s5m6/9M shows red over dangers in approach from east.
Suisnish Point pier head 2F.G(vert)
McMillan's Rock light buoy Fl(2)G.12s
Jackal Rock light buoy Fl.G.5s
Penfold Rock light buoy Fl.R.5s

At night

From east keep north of the red sector of Eyre Point light. In Caol Mor this light is obscured north of 063° but a direct course between Suisnish Pier and the west side of *McMillan's Rock* buoy clears all dangers.

There are no lights further north in the Sound of Raasay, but a mid-channel course can be estimated until Portree Harbour opens up. Look out for Sgeir Cnapach, described above.

Minor anchorages

Balmeanach Bay, 57°20'N 6°06'W, southwest of An Aird

Two underwater power cables cross to Raasay from a point marked by a pole two cables west of the southwest point of An Aird, and part of the bay is taken up by fish cages.

Holding has been found to be good.

Camas a' Mhor-bheoil, 57°20'·5N 6°06'·5W, lies west of the north point of An Aird.

Sgeir Dhubh, 3m high, lies 3½ cables northwest of the north point of An Aird, and a rock at the 2m contour ¼ mile from the head of the bay dries 0·8m.

Northerly swell sets into the bay.

Churchton Bay, Raasay, 57°21'N 6°05'W, southeast of Ardhuish.

A new ferry terminal and breakwater have been built at the NW end of Churchton Bay, incorporating Perch Rocks. Details of any lights have not yet been announced.

Visitors' moorings (blue buoys) are laid off the hotel east-southeast of the ferry terminal. Exposed southwest.

Portree

57°25'N 6°11'W

Westerly winds funnel fiercely out of Portree Harbour and down the sides of the hills making it difficult for a sailing boat to approach in these conditions. A short pontoon has been provided at the east end of the pier (see photo on next page). It is used by tenders from cruise liners, but yachts may be able to go alongside, on consulting the harbourmaster, for more or less brief periods.

Tides

Constant –0025 Ullapool (–0445 Dover)

Height in metres

MHWS	MHWN	MTL	MLWN	MLWS
5·3	3·7	2·9	1·9	0·7

Dangers and marks

Sgeir Mhor, a reef partly above water which extends a cable from a promontory on the north shore, ½ mile east of Portree Pier, is marked by a green conical light buoy.

Fish cages, together with a submerged rock, lie up to a cable off shore northeast of Sgeir Mhor.

A yellow conical light buoy about 1½ cables south-southeast of the pier, lies in 3m about a cable from the LW mark at the mouth of Loch Portree, the whole of which dries.

Lights

Sgeir Mhor light buoy Fl.G.5s
Yellow light buoy Fl.Y.5s
A light at the pier head, 2F.R(vert)6m4M

Portree. Visitors should not anchor among the moorings; visitors' moorings are laid at the north side of the bay

Anchorages

Much of the area northeast of the pier dries; a large area is occupied by moorings, marked by buoys, and anchoring there should be avoided.

The anchorage east of the pier in 7–10m is soft mud with not very good holding.

There are visitors' moorings off the north shore but these may be found untenable in a southerly wind owing to the fetch from Loch Portree.

The north side of the pier and stone slip dries almost completely at springs but a yacht may be able to go alongside temporarily at a suitable rise of tide; the sea level may be raised deceptively by the wind and there are small underwater obstructions at the slip. Dues are charged, although not for a brief visit, and crew should remain on board at all times to shift berth if necessary. It may be possible to remain at the pier overnight on Friday and Saturday nights.

Camas Ban, east of Vriskaig Point, is subject to severe downdraughts in southerly winds.

These downdraughts are known locally as 'whirlies' and, anywhere along the east side of Trotternish in strong southerlies, they can be seen spinning over the surface and sucking up a rotating cloud of spray.

Admiralty vessels sometimes use this anchorage but are unlikely to lie as far inshore as a yacht would anchor.

Supplies

Shops (supermarket, Dunvegan Road), Post Office, telephone, hotels, swimming pool (limited opening to public), showers at the Independent Hostel in The Square.

VI. SOUND OF RAASAY AND APPROACHES

Portree pier from north at low water

Portree. Landing pontoon at east end of the pier

Diesel, only in multiples of 10 gallons, from BP depot on the pier. Water from hose at pier. Petrol and diesel, *Calor Gas*, also mechanical repairs, at West End Garage (½ mile on Dunvegan Road).

Chandlery and hardware: North Skye Fishermen's Association on the pier, Bow and Stern and JansVans are both at Dunvegan Road.

Fladday Harbour

57°28'·5N 6°01'·3W

Southeast of Fladday Island on the west side of the north end of Raasay.

Charts
2209 (2210), (1:50,000)
OS map *24*

Tides
Constant –0025 Ullapool (–0445 Dover)
Height in metres

MHWS	MHWN	MTL	MLWN	MLWS
5·3	3·7	2·9	1·9	0·7

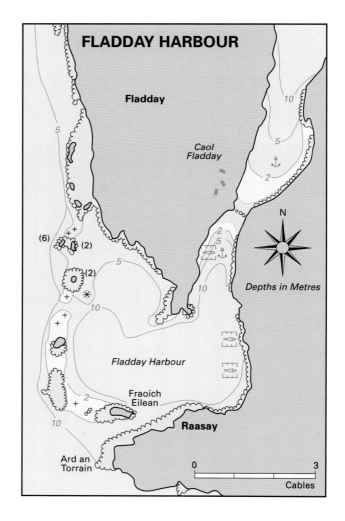

Fladday Harbour

Dangers and marks

Griana-sgeir, 7m high, together with a line of rocks, lie between ¼ and ½ mile west of Fladday.

Bo Leachan, south of Griana-sgeir, is cleared by keeping the west tangent of Rona open west of Griana-sgeir 018°.

Bo na Currachie, north of Griana-sgeir, is cleared by keeping the west tangent of Raasay open west of Griana-sgeir 201°.

At Manish Point, the south point of Loch Arnish, drying reefs extend more than a cable northwest.

The southwest side of the bay is enclosed by islets and drying rocks which, depending on the light, may be very difficult to distinguish; a few cottages on the shore of Loch Arnish may help to identify the way in.

Two cottages on Fladday show up well if there is any afternoon sunshine.

Directions

The entrance is about 60m wide between Ard an Torrain on Raasay and Fraoich Eilean ½ cable northwest of it, which must be identified before proceeding.

Drying reefs are said to extend part of the way across the passage from Ard an Torrain, but the depth in the northwest half of the passage is at least 6m.

After passing Fraoich Eilean head for the inlet between Fladday and Raasay.

Detached drying rocks, west-southwest of the south point of Fladday, shown on the plan in the previous *Pilot*, apparently do not exist, but the whole area should be treated with caution as there is no detailed survey.

A channel exists to the northwest, as shown, not less than 5m deep, but the only guidance is to identify the rocks on either side of it, the key being the 6m skerry. This passage should be taken on a heading of due east. Neither the passage to the north nor to the south of the recommended passage should be attempted. The passage east of Griana-sgeir is reported to have not less than 18m throughout.

The inlet is blocked ¼ mile from its mouth by boulders and a stone causeway which dry at low water; take care not to go too far in. Fish cages are moored on the east side of the harbour and this inlet is occupied by a permanently moored barge or work-boat.

The bottom appears to be stony with weed, but there is some clear sand under the cliffs of Fladday.

Caol Fladday (Fladday North Harbour) is the north part of the inlet between Fladday and Raasay. It is full of kelp and the holding is said to be poor.

Bo na Faochag at a depth of 1·8m lies 3½ cables north of Fladday; the summit of Beinn na h-Iolaire open east of Fladday 156° leads 1½ cables east of Bo na Faochag.

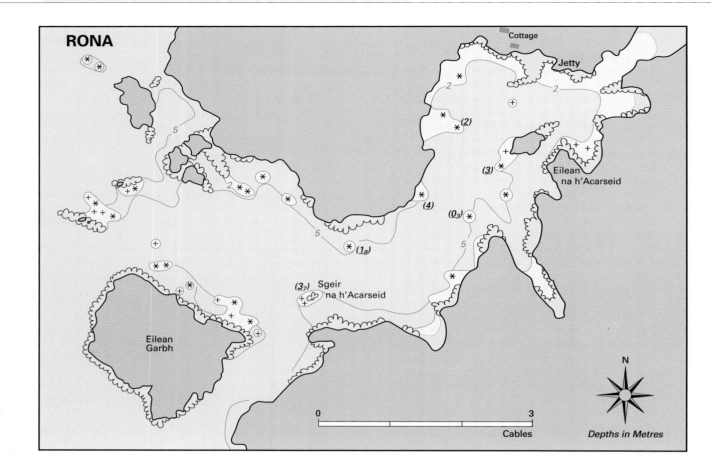

RONA

Cottage

Jetty

Eilean
na h'Acarseid

(2)

(3)

(4)

(0₃)

(1₈)

(3₇) Sgeir
na h'Acarseid

Eilean
Garbh

N

0   3

Cables   *Depths in Metres*

Caol Rona

⊕ East end 57°30'·3N 5°58'·5W

⊕ West end 57°31'·2N 6°00'W

Charts

2479 (1:18,000)
OS map Landranger 24; OS Explorer map 409

Tides

The southeast-going stream begins +0505 Ullapool
(+0045 Dover)

The northwest-going stream begins −0055 Ullapool
(−0515 Dover)

The spring rate is at least 2kns. The northwest-going
stream sets towards Eilean Seamraig.

Dangers and marks

Eilean an Fhraoich stands in the middle of the
channel with a beacon No. 4 on its southwest side.

Eilean Seamraig on the northeast side of the
channel is separated from Eilean Garbh by a channel
obstructed by rocks. Eilean Garbh is a tidal islet
joined to Rona by a stony isthmus.

A submerged rock lies ½ cable southwest of Eilean
an Fhraoich at a depth of 0·4m and a drying reef
extends ½ cable northwest.

No. 5 beacon stands on Rubha Ard Ghlaisen on
Raasay, nearly a mile south-southeast of Eilean an
Fhraoich.

A light beacon, No. 8, an orange and white
triangle, stands on the southeast point of Garbh
Eilean.

Eilean an Fhraoich can be passed on either side.

Lights

Rona lighthouse Fl.12s69m19M obscured 358°-050°
Ru na Lachan light beacon Oc.WR.8s21m10M, ¾ mile
    north of the Range Control building, shows red
    towards Caol Rona
Light beacon No. 8 Fl.3s8m5M

Acarseid Mhor, Rona

⊕ 57°31'·8N 6°00'W

A popular anchorage on the west side of Rona,
difficult to identify, as Eilean Garbh in the entrance
merges with the background, but a white arrow is
painted on the south side of the island to help
identification.

Survey information for Acarseid Mhor seems to be
under a spell and drying heights of rocks shown on
the plan are only approximate, or even positively
doubtful. Further observations will be gratefully
received.

Charts

2479 (1:18,000)
OS map Landranger 24; OS Explorer map 409

Acarseid Mhor, Rona

Tides

Constant –0025 Ullapool (–0445 Dover)

Height in metres

MHWS	MHWN	MTL	MLWN	MLWS
5·3	3·7	2·9	1·9	0·7

Directions

Approach southeast of Eilean Garbh and pass between Sgeir na h'Acarseid and the promontory close southeast of it. If the rock is covered, pass the promontory about 10m off on a line with the southeast tangent of Eilean Garbh astern; the rock shows pale below the water.

Steer for Eilean na h'Acarseid and, when within about a cable of it, alter course towards the cottage to pass west of the islet.

A rock at a depth of 0·7m was discovered the hard way some years ago, ½ cable north-northwest of Eilean na h'Acarseid.

In the passage north of Eilean Garbh there are no reference points, but rocks on either side of the passage are usually marked by swell breaking on them.

Anchorage

Anchor northwest or northeast of Eilean na h'Acarseid clear of drying reefs as shown.

Holding is poor in places, consisting of soft black mud well ploughed by yachts' anchors.

There is said to be space to anchor west of the reef west of the jetty.

The anchorage formerly shown just east of the drying rock in the entrance has a rocky bottom, and submerged rocks lie close enough to the surface to embarass a yacht.

A pontoon is provided at the jetty for supply boats for the island, and care should be taken that dinghies do not obstruct them.

Toilets and showers and washing machines are provided at Rona Lodge. Water may be available.

Acarseid Mhor, Rona

Loch a' Bhraige

⊕ 57°35'N 6°59'W

Chart

2534 (1:7,500)

This inlet is used by the Admiralty and is elaborately marked and lit, providing a harbour, if needed, when coming from the north of Skye after dark but it has little other attraction for a yacht.

Directions

Sgeir Shuas is a group of islets on the north side of the entrance, on one of which is a light beacon.

A drying rock lies ¾ cable southwest of the north point of the loch, otherwise it is clean to near the head of the inlet where a reef, partly above water, with light beacon No. 9 on it, extends 1½ cables northwest from the shore.

The inlet in the northeast corner, where there is a piled quay with rubber fendering, gives good shelter. Admiralty vessels often lie at the quay overnight.

Pass either side of the detached light beacon and anchor in the northeast inlet clear of the approach to the quay.

Alternative anchorages are either side of the reef on which beacon No. 9 stands; a mooring buoy is laid south of the reef.

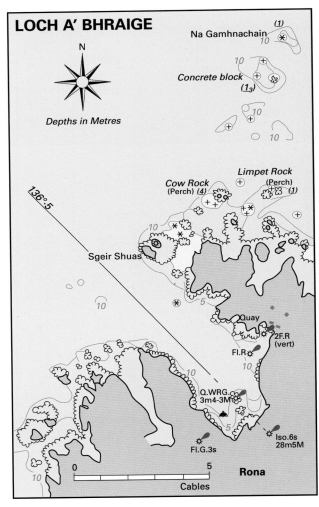

Lights

Rona lighthouse Fl.12s69m19M obscd 358°- 050°
Sgeir Shuas light beacon Fl.R.2s6m3M
No. 9 light beacon Q.WRG.3m4-3M
No. 10 light beacon Iso.6s28m5M
Detached light beacon off NE inlet Fl.R.5s4m3M
Quay, southwest corner 2F.R(vert)
No. 1 light beacon Fl.G.3s91m3M

At night

Light beacons No. 9 and No. 10 in line lead into the loch 136·5°.

Passage at the North end of Rona

Dangers and marks

Rocks, submerged and drying, extend eight cables north of Rona to Na Gamhnachain which dries 1m.

A rock 1½ cables south of Na Gamhnachain has a concrete block built up on it which dries 1·3m.

Several submerged rocks lie between Na Gamhnachain and Rona.

Cow Rock, 4m high, two cables north of the northwest point of Rona, and Limpet Rock, one metre high and two cables further east, both have perches on them.

A submerged rock at a depth of 1·8m lies ½ cable north of a direct line between these two rocks, apart from which the nearest charted hazard is a submerged rock two cables north of Cow Rock. An inshore passage north of these rocks may be taken in clear settled weather.

North card light buoy, Q, has been established north of Na Gamhnachain.

Staffin Bay from southeast

Northeast Skye

Rubha na h-Aiseig is the northeast point, and Rubha Hunish the northwest point of Trotternish, the north peninsula of Skye.

Eilean Trodday, a grassy flat-topped island, with a light beacon on its centre, lies nearly a mile north of Rubha na h-Aiseig.

The west side of Skye is described in *Chapter III.*

Charts

2210 (1:50,000)
OS Landranger map 23

Tides

Tidal streams round the north end of Skye follow the coast with eddies in the bays between headlands.

Heavy overfalls occur between Rubha na h-Aiseig and Staffin Bay.

In the passage between Rubha na h-Aiseig on Skye and Eilean Trodday the spring rate is 2½kns.

The east-going stream begins –0350 Ullapool (+0415 Dover)

The west-going stream begins +0235 Ullapool (–0145 Dover)

Off Rubha Hunish the spring rate is 2½kns.

The northeast-going stream begins –0405 Ullapool (+0400 Dover)

The southwest-going stream begins +0220 Ullapool (–0200 Dover)

Lights

Eilean Trodday Fl(2)WRG.10s49m12-9M
Rona Fl.12s69m19M 358°-obscd-050°

Minor anchorages

Staffin Bay, 57°38'·5N 6°13'W, is a clean open bay exposed northeast and subject to squalls in westerly winds. Eilean Floddigarry provides some shelter from the north.

Clach nan Ramh, two cables off Skye seven cables north-northwest of Eilean Flodigarry, north of Staffin Bay, dries 3·8m. If approaching or leaving by the passage between Skye and Eilean Flodigarry, when beyond the north end of Flodigarry keep Staffin Island hidden behind Eilean Flodigarry 153° to clear this rock.

Anchor either on the east side of the bay or in its southwest corner.

The passage between Staffin Island and Skye is blocked by rocks.

A shop and restaurant stand on the main road ½ mile from Quiraing Lodge, the large house at the mouth of a burn on the south side of the bay.

Kilmaluag Bay, 57°41'·5N 6°18'W, a small inlet ¾ mile south of Rubha na h-Aiseig, is convenient for waiting for suitable conditions for a passage beyond the north end of Skye or as an overnight anchorage in settled weather, although the bottom is stony in places and the anchor chain may grumble.

A drying reef extends more than 1½ cables from the south point of the entrance. The bay is subject to fierce squalls in strong westerly winds.

VII. Northwest mainland – Rubha Reidh to Point of Stoer

Passage notes – Rubha Reidh to Loch Inchard

⊕ Two miles west of Rubha Reidh 51°57′·6N 5°52′W

⊕ One mile NW of Point of Stoer 57°16′·5N 5°25′W

The 40 miles of coast from Rubha Reidh to Loch Inchard is deeply indented, consisting of great bays between impressive headlands, with almost no continuous length of coastline facing seaward.

Two of the headlands, Rubha Reidh and Point of Stoer, are notorious for heavy seas, caused mainly by their exposure and the strength of the tidal streams around them.

Seas around these headlands are particularly dangerous with wind against tide and they should be given a berth of several miles if it is necessary to pass them under such conditions.

Charts

1794, 1785 (1:100,000)
OS Landranger maps 19, 15, 9;
OS Explorer maps 434, 435, 439, 442

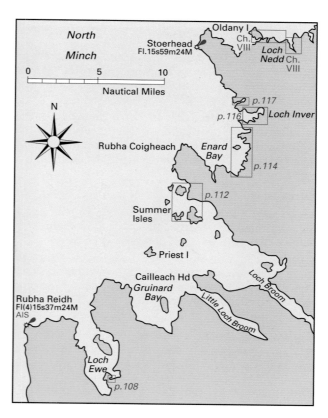

Tides at Rubha Reidh

The northeast-going stream begins –0335 Ullapool (+0430 Dover)

The southwest-going stream begins +0305 Ullapool (–0115 Dover)

The spring rate of these streams is 3kns. There may be eddies inshore on the downstream side of the point.

At Rubha Coigeach and Point of Stoer:

The north-going stream begins –0250 Ullapool (+0515 Dover)

The south-going stream begins +0420 Ullapool (HW Dover)

The spring rate of these streams is 2½kns.

Dangers and marks

Rubha Reidh, 57°52′N 5°48′W, is marked by a white lighthouse 25m in height, and a conspicuous radio mast stands on a hill 1½ miles southeast of the point.

Point of Stoer is a bold headland with a stack, the Old Man of Stoer, 56m in height, on its northwest side, which shows very distinctly from northeast. Stoerhead lighthouse, a white tower 14m in height stands on a cliff 1¾ miles south-southwest of the point.

Lights

Rubha Reidh Fl(4)15s37m24M
Soyea Island (Loch Inver) Fl(2)10s34m6M
Stoerhead Fl.15s59m24M
Rubha na Leacaig (Loch Inchard) Fl(2)10s30m8M
Tiumpan Head (Lewis) Fl(2)15s55m25M
Cape Wrath lighthouse Fl(4)30s122m24M is obscured east of 025°

At night, in clear moderate weather, these lights will be sufficient for a passage along the coast.

Shelter

Loch Torridon, Gairloch, Isle of Ewe in Loch Ewe, Summer Isles, Loch Inver, various lochs on the south side of Eddrachillis Bay, Loch Laxford, Kinlochbervie; all provide some shelter during a passage along the coast.

Loch Ewe

57°51′N 5°40′W

Charts

2509 (1:25,000) approach only, 3146 (1:12,500)
OS Landranger map 19

Tides

Off the entrance, tidal streams run at up to 2½kns.
The NNE-going stream begins –0335 Ullapool
(+0430 Dover)
The SSW-going stream begins +0305 Ullapool
(–0115 Dover)
Within the loch, streams turn at HW and LW and may
reach 1kn in narrower passages.
Constant –0010 Ullapool (–0430 Dover)
Height in metres

MHWS	MHWN	MTL	MLWN	MLWS
5·1	3·8	2·9	2·0	0·7

Directions

The entrance lies four miles east of Rubha Reidh and
has no hidden dangers.

Fairway buoy (RW) and No. 1 green conical light
buoy are in the fairway.

Isle of Ewe, two miles long, is near the east shore
of the loch, and Sgeir an Araig, 12m high, is ½ mile
northwest of Isle of Ewe.

The passage round the south end of Isle of Ewe is
marked by three red can light buoys.

A NATO fuelling jetty is on the mainland east-
southeast of the Isle of Ewe.

Greenstone Point, 3½ miles north-northeast of the
entrance to Loch Ewe, produces heavy seas with
wind against tide.

Lights

Fairway light buoy LFl.10s
No. 1 light buoy Fl(3)G.10s
Red light buoys east of Ewe Island:
D (south) Fl(2)R.10s
E (middle) Fl.R.2s
F (north) Fl(4)R.10s
NATO fuelling jetty and dolphins north and south each
  Fl.G.4s

Anchorages

Several bays on the west side of the loch provide an
occasional overnight anchorage to save going further
up the loch.

Acarseid nan Uamh, one mile south-southwest of
the Fairway buoy, has been found satisfactory in
settled weather.

Acarseid Mhor, 57°50'·6N 5°38'W, sometimes known
as Camas Angus, on the east side of the north end of
Isle of Ewe, is clean apart from a drying reef on its
south side and has been found to give good shelter
and holding in gales between south and northwest.

A mooring and small fish cages lie in the mouth of
the bay.

Aultbea, 57°50'·3N 5°3'·5W, on the east side of the
sound is partly sheltered by Aird Point on which
there is a stone pier which dries alongside, with a
decaying timber-piled pier head.

Much of the bay inshore of the pier dries or is
shoal, with moorings for inshore fishing boats.

Anchor off a hotel on the east shore, or close east
of the pier for some protection from northwest.

In west or southwest winds, Acarseid Mhor gives
better shelter.

Supplies

Shop (Bridgend Stores, chart agent and *Calor Gas*),
butcher ¼ mile. Post Office, telephone, hotels, water
tap at pier. Petrol (but not diesel) at Forbes Garage,
which can help with mechanical and electrical
repairs in an emergency.

Loch Thurnaig, 57°47'·5N 5°35'W, two miles south
of Isle of Ewe.

The bottom is soft mud with some rock, but
shelter may be found in Ob na Ba Ruaidhe in the
southwest corner behind a drying reef which extends
from the north side of the entrance to this bay.

The bottom is partly rocky and partly very soft
mud.

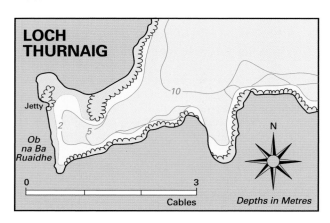

Camas Glas, 57°46'·7N 5°36'·5W, is an occasional
anchorage from which to visit Inverewe Gardens.

Anchor off a stone jetty on the north side of
Creagan nan Cudaigean, a wooded rocky
promontory on the east side of the head of the loch,
½ mile north of Poolewe and the trees mop up winds
from most directions.

Good holding is found south of the promontory at
Port na Cloiche Gile well offshore, but the head of
the bay dries off and the depth should be checked
carefully.

Poolewe, at the southwest corner of the head of the
loch, provides fair shelter in southwesterly winds.

Boor Rocks, one mile northwest of Poolewe, stand
up to 3m above water with drying rocks more than a
cable further northwest.

Supplies

Shop, Post Office, telephone, hotel. Petrol, *Calor
Gas* and diesel at garage (which will also help with
small engineering repairs). Swimming pool.

Gruinard Bay has no regular anchorages, although
there are moderate depths in places around its shore
and a jetty at Laide on the southwest side of the bay.
Rocks are adequately shown on chart *1794*.

Shop and Post Office.

Cailleach Head, at the east side of Gruinard Bay 15
miles east-northeast of Rubha Reidh, is marked by a
6m-high white light beacon at a height of 55m.

Little Loch Broom

57°54′N 5°22′W

Charts

2500 (1:25,000)
OS Landranger map 19; OS Explorer map 439

South of Cailleach Head, Ardross Rock lies four cables east-northeast of the south point of the entrance in a depth of 0·6m; the loch is otherwise clean but provides little shelter and the head dries off for ½ mile.

Anchor on the south side, about 1½ miles from the head of the loch at Camusnagaul, east of a slight promontory about a mile east-southeast of a conspicuous fish farm.

Alternatively, in northerly winds, off the jetty at Scoraig, one mile within the north side of the entrance.

The entrance is now marked by lights, Fl.R.5s2M at Scoraig, and Fl.G.5s2M on the south shore.

Supplies

Hotel, telephone at Dundonnell at head of the loch.

Loch Broom

57°55′·N 5°15′W

Charts

2500 (1:25,000)
OS Landranger map 19; OS Explorer map 439

Tides

Streams are weak within the loch but reach 1kn in the narrows southeast of Ullapool.

The in-going stream begins −0555 Ullapool (+0210 Dover)

The out-going stream begins +0005 Ullapool (−0415 Dover)

Constant 0000 Ullapool (−0420 Dover)

Height in metres

MHWS	MHWN	MTL	MLWN	MLWS
5·2	3·9	3·0	2·1	0·7

Dangers and marks

A rock 1m high lies a cable off Leac Dhonn, 1½ miles east-northeast of Cailleach Head.

Rubha Cadail, 4½ miles further east, marked by a white light beacon 9m in height, is on the north side of the entrance to Loch Broom.

Ullapool Point, 57°53′·6N 5°10′W, is on the northeast side of the loch, 2½ miles southeast of Rubha Cadail.

A red can light buoy four cables northwest of Ullapool Point marks shoal water at the mouth of a river.

Ullapool pier is two cables northeast of the point.

Ullapool

Ullapool was founded by the British Fisheries Society in 1788, and is able to provide or arrange for most services.

A large car ferry runs from Ullapool to Stornoway on Lewis.

Lights

Cailleach Head Fl(2)12s60m9M
Rubha Cadail light beacon Fl.WRG.6s11m9-6M
Light buoy northwest of Ullapool Point Q.R
Ullapool Point Iso.R.4s8m6M
Pier 2F.R(vert)

Mooring and anchorage

Yachts can go alongside the east end, or inside the eastern arm of the pier for a short time but the depth there should be watched and some crew must stay on board at all times to move the boat if necessary to let fishing boats in or out.

Eight moorings for visiting yachts are provided off the slip east of the pier. Before going alongside the quay or adjacent landing pontoon on its north side, yachts must consult the harbourmaster.

Ullapool

Acarseid Driseach from Tanera Mor

Caolas Eilean Ristol from southwest

Many moorings lie east of the piers; there is space to anchor among them but yachts must keep clear of the approach to the piers; there is a lot of rubbish on the bottom and a tripping line is essential.

Some moorings are not maintained and some are in frequent use and local advice should be sought before using one.

Supplies

Shops (one of which usually opens on Sunday), Post Office, telephone, banks, hotels, petrol and diesel at garage, water hoses at pier. *Calor Gas* at supermarket at West Argyll Street, one block back from the pier. Marine engineers and divers at the pier: For advice on all services, ask harbourmaster ☎ 01854 612091, VHF Ch 14, 16.

An ATM located inside the CalMac waiting rooms at the ferry terminal can be accessed during normal port opening hours.

Minor anchorages – Loch Broom and approaches

Loch Kanaird, 57°57'N 5°12'W, east of Isle Martin, about a mile northeast of Rubha Cadail.

Entrance by the north side of the island is straightforward.

In the south entrance, drying spits extend from both sides leaving a passage ½ cable wide with no satisfactory leading line except to keep the east tangent of Isle Martin bearing 358°.

Drying rocks lie between Aird na h-Eighe, the southeast point of the bay, and Sgeir Mhor, a rock 1m high, about two cables north of the point.

There are fish cages and moorings but space will usually be found either in the bight on the east shore of Isle Martin or off Ardmair on the southeast side of the bay.

A pontoon has been established in the bight on the east side of Isle Martin, with a light Fl.G.8s on its end.

Annat Bay (Feith an Fheoir), two miles east of Cailleach Head. Anchor in the mouth of an inlet at the west end of the bay.

Altnaharrie, on the southwest side of the loch opposite Ullapool Point; moorings may be available overnight. Hotel and restaurant.

Loggie Bay, 57°52'N 5°07'W, on the southwest side of the loch immediately beyond the narrows 1½ miles southeast of Ullapool Point. Fish-farming rafts and moorings restrict the space.

Summer Isles

58°01'N 5°25'W

The name applies to the group of about 30 islands scattered over the approaches to Loch Broom, but only Tanera Mor and Tanera Beg on the north side have anchorages which are at all sheltered.

Priest Island, the most southwesterly of the group, has a bay on its northeast side only suitable as an occasional anchorage in settled weather. The bottom consists mainly of boulders.

This island was held for a time by French government forces during the Jacobite rising of 1745.

Charts

2501 (1:26,000)
OS map Landranger 15

Tides

Constant –0005 Ullapool (–0425 Dover)
Height in metres

MHWS	MHWN	MTL	MLWN	MLWS
5·1	4·0	3·0	2·1	0·8

Dangers and marks

Most rocks are above water but there are drying rocks in Dorney Sound, north of Tanera Mor and Tanera Beg, in Horse Sound and south of Horse Island.

In Dorney Sound north of Tanera Mor, Iolla a Mealan, which dries 0·8m, is avoided by keeping the south point of Eilean Mullagrach just open south of Isle Ristol 297°.

On the south side of the sound, Sgeir Iasgaich, which dries 3·7m three cables east of Sgeir Dubh, is clear of the fairway but should be watched for.

Sgeir a Chapuill, a cable north of Tanera Mor, dries 2·3m.

In Horse Sound, Iolla Beg and Mary Rock are drying rocks ¼ mile off Rubha Dubh Ard at the southeast point of the sound.

They are cleared by keeping the northeast tangent of Meall nan Gabhar at the north end of Horse Island in line with Rubha Dunan, the point of the mainland to the north, and the summit of Meall an Fheadain 331°.

The north end of Stac Mhic Aonghais open south of Horse Island 283° leads south of Iolla Beg.

Iolla Mhor, two cables south of Horse Island, dries 3·9m.

Stac Mhic Aonghais   Horse Island

Stac Mhic Aonghais (Angus Stac) 283° open to the south of Horse Island clears Iolla Beg

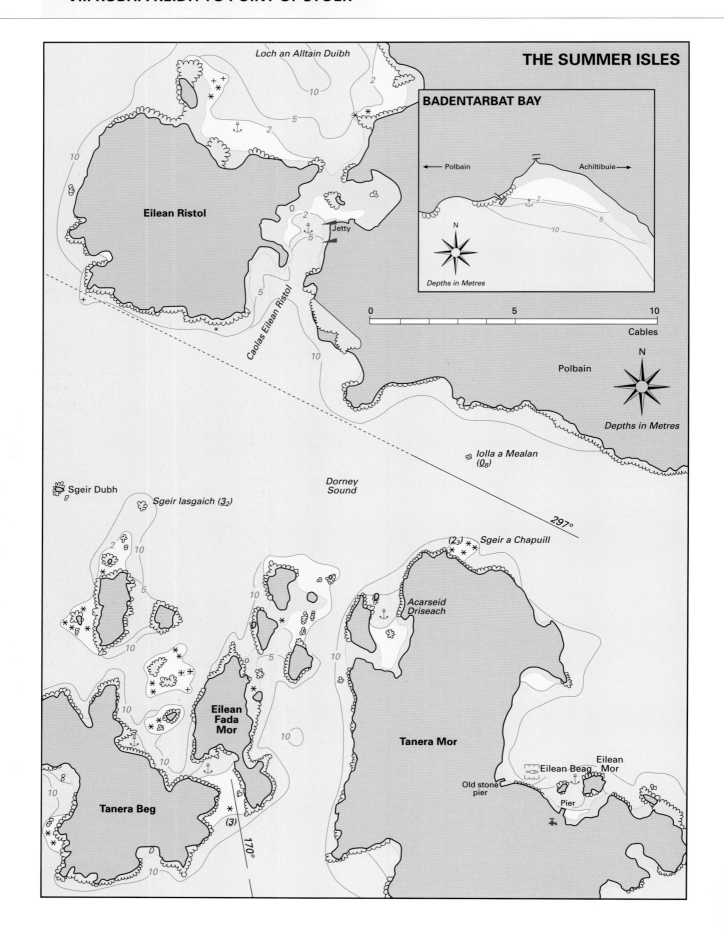

THE SUMMER ISLES

Loch an Alltain Duibh

Eilean Ristol

Caolas Eilean Ristol

Jetty

BADENTARBAT BAY

← Polbain

Achiltibuie →

N

Depths in Metres

0   5   10

Cables

N

Polbain

Depths in Metres

Iolla a Mealan
(0_8)

Dorney
Sound

297°

Sgeir Dubh

Sgeir Iasgaich (3_2)

Sgeir a Chapuill

(2_3)

Acarseid
Driseach

Eilean
Fada
Mor

Tanera Mor

Eilean Beag

Eilean
Mor

Old stone
pier

Pier

Tanera Beg

(3)

170°

Anchorages

Achiltibuie Anchor east-southeast of pier on the northwest side of Badentarbat Bay, but not further inshore as it is shoal.

Hotel and shops nearby; Polbain Stores (northwest) and Sinclair Stores (southeast), which also stocks *Calor Gas*, each about 10 minutes' walk in opposite directions. Post Office at Achiltibuie.

Tanera Mor The Anchorage on the east side of the island is generally deep and obstructed by fish cages.

The Cabbage Patch, between Eilean Beag and Eilean Mor on the south side of the bay, is full of moorings, although a small boat might anchor close inshore.

There is a good modern pier where a boat might dry out for repairs. Water at the pier.

Acarseid Driseach at the northwest corner of Tanera Mor, on the east side of Eilean na Saile, is shoal and full of weed.

A drying rock lies in the middle of the south end of the inlet.

The approach from the south by Caolas Mhill Gharbh (and north of Eilean na Saile) is straightforward.

Tanera Beg has several sheltered anchorages on its northeast side, but these are noted as being subject to strong tide and thick kelp.

Approach from north keeping ¼ cable off the west side of Eilean Fada Mor to avoid rocks submerged and awash on the west side of the channel.

Floats and fishing nets may be laid in this channel. From south it is possible in quiet weather to approach above half tide by the passage between the east end of Tanera Beg and Eilean Fada Mor, in which the least depth is charted as 0·8m with two rocks which dry at least 3m.

Tanera Beag and Eilean Fada Mor. Note the rocks which are submerged in this photo

The passage between the drying rock in the middle of the south entrance and reefs at the south end of Eilean Fada Mor is only ½ cable wide.

Steer to pass ¼ cable from the east side of the passage heading 360° and as soon as the west end of the passage opens alter course to pass close northeast of the east point of Tanera Beg.

A line astern for this passage, Cailleach Head lighthouse over the left tangent of Eilean Dubh 170°, has been found to lead between the rocks in this passage.

Caolas Eilean Ristol, 58°02'·5N 5°25'·5W. Anchor off the slip clear of moorings, and show an anchor light as fishing boats come in after dark. Light on end of the slip Fl.G.3s.

Shop at Polbain two miles.

Loch an Alltain Duibh, north of Eilean Ristol, provides occasional anchorage off the north shore of Eilean Ristol.

For passage notes see the beginning of this chapter.

Enard Bay

There are several moderately sheltered inlets on the east side of the bay, with offshore islands that give some further shelter, but none can be particularly recommended.

Charts

2504 (1:25,000)
OS map Landranger 15; OS Explorer map 442

Tides

Streams are insignificant in Enard Bay.
Constant –0005 Ullapool (–0425 Dover)
Height in metres

MHWS	MHWN	MTL	MLWN	MLWS
5·0	3·9	3·0	2·1	0·8

Dangers and marks

Detached drying rocks lie up to two cables off the shore, both of the mainland and of various islands. These are shown on chart *1794* but, for exploring, inshore chart *2504* must be used.

Eilean Mor, the highest island in Enard Bay, four miles east of Rubha Coigeach and ½ mile offshore, is a useful reference point.

Lights

Soyea Island (Loch Inver) Fl(2)10s34m6M
Stoerhead Fl.15s59m24M

Anchorages

Achnahaird Bay, 58°04'N 5°21'·5W, on the south side of Enard Bay, has a fine sandy beach, but is too exposed for all but an occasional daytime anchorage.

Camas a' Bhothain, 58°05'N 5°21'W, close east of Achnahaird Bay, is named Sandy Bay on old charts, but fails to live up to this name as the bottom consists of boulders and holding is poor.

A drying reef extends north from Rubha Beag at the west side of the bay towards Black Rock which

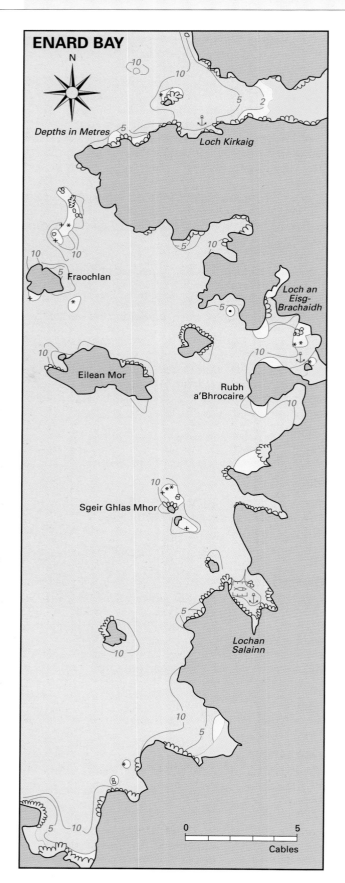

ENARD BAY

N

Depths in Metres

Loch Kirkaig

Fraochlan

Loch an Eisg-Brachaidh

Eilean Mor

Rubh a'Bhrocaire

Sgeir Ghlas Mhor

Lochan Salainn

0   5
Cables

dries, one cable north of a rock which does not cover, on the reef.

The entrance is between this reef and rocks which extend ½ cable west of Sgeir Bhuidhe in the middle of the bay.

Lochan Salainn, 58°05′N 5°17′W, is probably the best anchorage in Enard Bay. It is not named on some charts but lies about a mile southeast of Eilean Mor.

Islets extend northwest from its entrance to Sgeir Ghlas Mhor and Bheag which have drying rocks up to one cable north of them and a submerged rock ½ cable southeast.

A drying rock lies more than ½ cable from the northeast side of the inlet and there are some fish cages.

Loch an Eisg-Brachaidh, 58°06′·3N 5°16′·5W, ¾ mile east of Eilean Mor, is sheltered by several islands. Several rocks within are not shown on uncorrected copies of the current chart (*see plan*).

A drying rock lies ¾ cable southeast of Fraochlan, the island north of Eilean Mor, and more drying rocks lie in the middle of the passage north of Fraochlan.

Approach by either side of Eilean Mor, but if by the north side keep closer to Eilean Mor.
Anchor close to the northeast side of Rubh a' Bhrocaire at the south side of the bay.

Loch Kirkaig, 58°07′·5N 5°17′W, ¾ mile southeast of Kirkaig Point at the entrance to Loch Inver, provides some shelter close to the south shore.

Loch Inver

58°09′N 5°15′W

A breakwater provides good shelter, with pontoons for yachts up to 12m. The harbour is used by Breton fishing boats up to 50m in length.

Tides

Constant –0005 Ullapool (–0425 Dover)
Height in metres

MHWS	MHWN	MTL	MLWN	MLWS
5·0	3·9	3·0	2·1	0·8

Dangers and marks

Soyea Island lies ½ mile off the entrance to the loch.

A submerged rock lies two cables north of its east end at a depth of 0·2m and drying reefs up to two cables northeast of its east point.

Bo Caolas, which dries 3·2m, three cables northeast of the east point of the island, has a beacon with a cage topmark at its west end.

Glas Leac, 1¼ miles east of Soyea Island, is a small grass-topped islet 6m high with drying reefs and shoals up to ½ cable north of it.

Drying rocks lie more than a cable off the north shore north of Glas Leac, and off the east point of Camas na Frithearaich, ½ mile northwest of the islet.

Most of the bays on the south side of the loch are occupied by moorings and some have drying rocks in them.

Loch Kirkaig

Lochinver

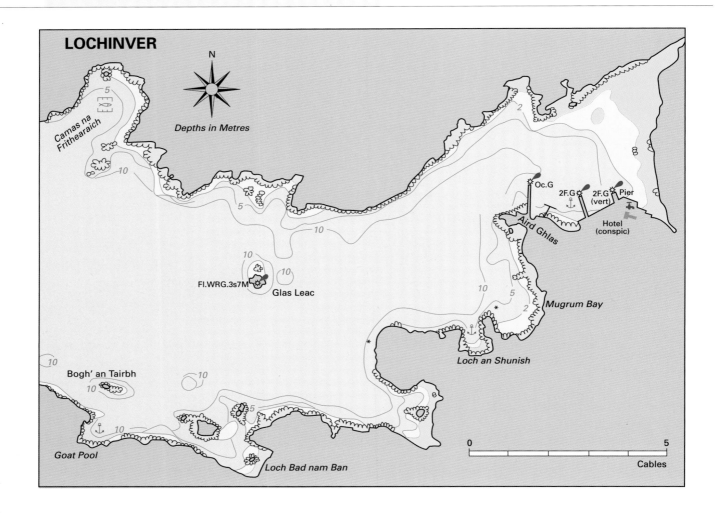

LOCHINVER

Lights

Soyea Island Fl(2)10s34m6M
Glas Leac Fl.WRG.3s7m
Breakwater Q.G.3m1M
Finger Jetty 2F.G(vert)
Pier head 2F.G(vert)

At night

Glas Leac light beacon shows white over the fairways, both north and south of Soyea Island, but the south passage is cleaner; a white sector also shows eastward towards the harbour.

Minor anchorages

Goat Pool, 58°08′·3N 5°17′W, ½ mile east of Kirkaig Point, is deep and the bottom is rocky until close in.

Pass either side of Bogh' an Tairbh which is only 0·3m high with drying reefs ½ cable east of it.

Loch Bad nam Ban, 58°08′·25N 5°16′·4W, has enough moorings to make it difficult to find space to anchor.

Lochinver

The head of the breakwater lies six cables east of Glas Leac.

Visiting yachts are requested to contact the harbourmaster by VHF before entering harbour. Watch is kept, although not 24hr, on Ch 16 and 09.

Pontoons are provided for small craft (up to 12m) between the breakwater and the Finger Jetty.

Yachts should not be left unattended alongside fixed jetties or quays. Wherever berthed consult the harbourmaster immediately.

Supplies

Shops (shop at the pier open in evenings when fishing boats come in).

Baker, Post Office, telephone, hotel.

Petrol at garage, diesel and water at pier.

Fishermen's chandlery; *Calor Gas* at chandlery. A concrete slip beyond the Culag Pier may be available to dry out for underwater repairs.

Lochinver, with pontoons for small craft

Loch Roe

Loch Roe

58°10′N 5°18′W

The entrance lies one mile north of Soyea Island.

Pool Bay which provides the best shelter may be fully occupied by moorings.

Dangers and marks

Bo Burrick, ½ cable north-northwest of Rubha Rodha, the south point of the entrance, dries 4·1m.

McAllister Rock ¼ cable off the north side of the entrance channel, dries 2·1m.

About six cables northeast of Rubha Rodha, two tidal islets, about 4m high, lie northeast of a promontory which extends northeast from the south shore, sheltering the anchorage at Pool Bay.

Drying reefs extend 20–30m east of the islets.

Bo Pool, which dries 1·7m, lies less than ½ cable further east.

Submerged rocks may lie at the sides of the channel.

Approach either when Bo Pool is showing or when the tide has risen enough to pass safely over it and anchor in Pool Bay, south of the islets.

East of Bo Pool a sill with drying rocks on it lies across the loch, but it is possible, with great care, to pass further up the loch. Inshore fishing boats are moored in various inlets around the loch.

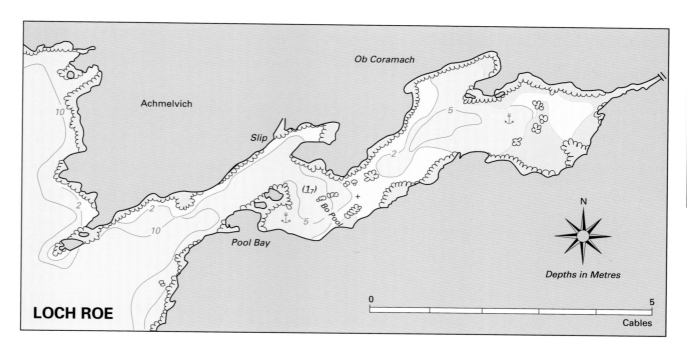

LOCH ROE

VIII. Northwest mainland – Point of Stoer to Cape Wrath

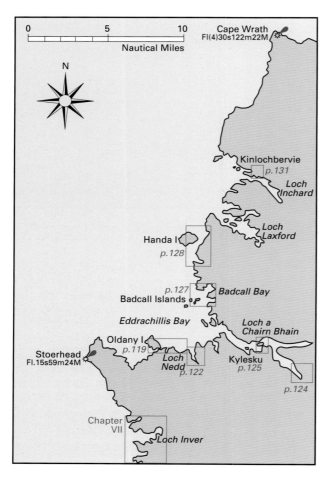

Eddrachillis Bay

Between Point of Stoer and Handa Island is an entertaining collection of islands and lochs, well worth the effort of getting there.

No general directions are necessary other than the passage notes on page 107 and a reminder of the heavy seas to be expected at Point of Stoer.

Charts

2502 (1:25,000) is essential for exploring the area in any detail
OS Landranger maps 15, 9; OS Explorer maps 445, 446

Tides

Except in Kylesku, streams are insignificant in Eddrachillis Bay.
Constant 0000 Ullapool (–0420 Dover)
Height in metres

MHWS	MHWN	MTL	MLWN	MLWS
4·9	3·7	2·8	1·9	0·7

Anchorages

Clashnessie Bay, between Point of Stoer and Oldany Island, has no regular anchorage, but several bays and inlets might be rewarding to explore on a quiet day. It may be possible for a Drascombe Lugger or similar to negotiate the passage south of Oldany Island – on a rising tide.

Culkein Drumbeg, 58°15'·2N 5°14'W, is a landlocked pool east of Oldany Island with rocks awash in the entrance which make the approach difficult, although they can often be seen breaking.

Follow the plan closely.

Pass about a cable northeast of Eilean nan Uan and steer 160° as if to pass clear west of Eilean na Cille, but look out for the rock awash north of Eilean nam Boc.

When the north side of Eilean nam Boc comes abeam steer to starboard to pass ¼ cable off its east point and avoid the drying reef on the east side of the channel.

Hold on toward the south side of the inlet before turning east to avoid a rock which dries 3m southwest of Eilean na Cille, and if heading further east keep toward one side or the other to avoid a rock which dries 0·9m in mid-channel.

The head of the jetty just dries. Water tap at jetty.

Loch Dhrombaig, 58°15'N 5°12'W, is straightforward to approach except for a submerged rock ½ cable west of the 15m islet north of the west entrance.

Anchor off shingle beach at southeast side of the pool.

In the east entrance to the loch the least depth is 1·8m.

Submerged rocks lie one cable offshore ½ mile further east.

Drying rocks lie west and southwest of Sgeir Liath, the outermost islet northeast of Loch Dhrombaig.

Shop, Post Office, telephone, hotel. Advice and assistance may be sought from Drumbeg Charters at the hotel, ☎ 01571 833236.

Loch Nedd, 58°15'N 5°10'W, can be safely approached in heavy northerly weather and provides good shelter.

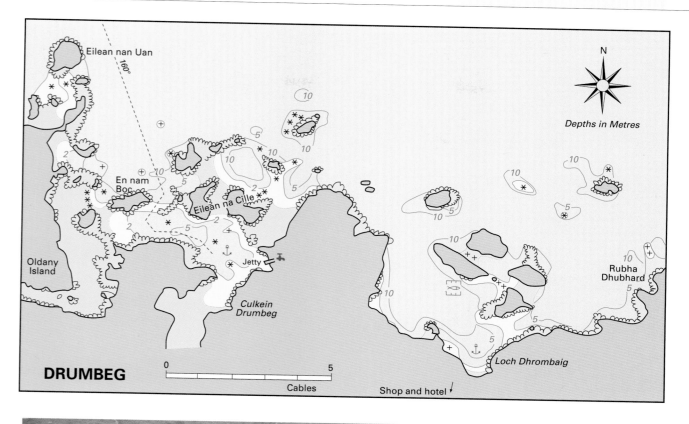

DRUMBEG

Depths in Metres

Eilean nan Uan

En nam Boc

Eilean na Cille

Oldany Island

Culkein Drumbeg

Jetty

Rubha Dhubhard

Loch Dhrombaig

Shop and hotel

Cables

Culkein Drumbeg from west-northwest

VIII. POINT OF STOER TO CAPE WRATH

Culkein Drumbeg entrance. Note the track of the fishing boat, and the rock breaking off the north point of Eilean nam Boc

Culkein Drumbeg

Loch Dhrombaig from north-northwest

Loch Nedd

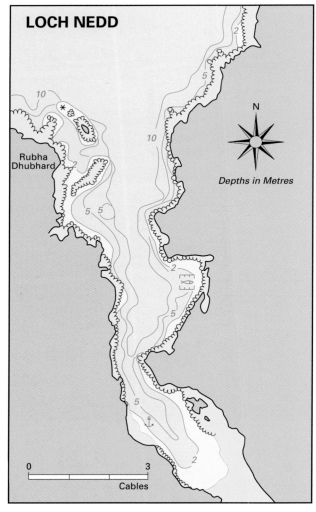

LOCH NEDD

Rubha Dhubhard

Depths in Metres

N

Cables

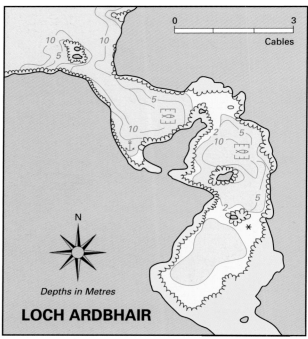

N

Depths in Metres

LOCH ARDBHAIR

Cables

Kerrachar Bay

Drying reefs extend almost halfway across the entrance from the west side and up to a cable north of Rubha Dhubhard.

Many moorings lie in the inner loch and the head dries off for ¼ mile.

Loch Ardbhair, 58°15′N 5°07′W, is cluttered with rocks, and even the outer part of this loch is occupied by fish cages and floats, but there is some space to anchor.

Pass east of the reef in the mouth of the loch, which does not usually cover, and anchor in the southwest corner of the outer loch.

Four cables beyond the reef at the entrance the loch is almost completely blocked by drying rocks where the tide runs strongly, although a way through can be found.

Further in there are more fish cages.

South of an islet another reef occupies most of the middle of the loch and the head of the loch dries off ¼ mile, but anyone who has penetrated this far may find a clear anchorage under the west shore.

Loch a' Chairn Bhain

58°16′·5N 5°07′W

This loch is entered between Rubha nam Fias, on the south shore five miles east of Oldany Island, and the Calbha islands.

Ravens Rock, ¼ mile south of Calbha Beag, dries 1·8m and Lachen Shoal four cables west-southwest of Calbha Beag, at a depth of 2·1m, breaks heavily in gales.

Several inlets on the north side of the entrance remain unexplored.

Loch Shark, 58°16′·8N 5°06′·3W, the most easterly of these, has a submerged rock in the middle of its entrance, which is only ¼ cable wide.

Kerrachar Bay, four cables south-southeast of Rubha na Fias, is an occasional anchorage, off a

Loch Nedd

Loch Ardbhair

house on the shore. Reefs extend more than ½ cable from the north point of the bay, and the bottom has been found to be thick with weed.

Loch a' Chairn Bhain runs in a southeasterly direction for four miles to Kylesku (Caolas Cumhann) a narrow passage where the tide runs strongly with eddies on each side. An elegant concrete bridge and power cables cross the narrows, both with 24m headroom.

Tides

At Kylesku run at up to 2½kns;
The in-going stream begins –0545 Ullapool (+0220 Dover).
The out-going stream begins +0040 Ullapool (–0340 Dover).

Lights

Q.R.24m3M lights are shown from the north bridge supports on both sides, and Q.G.24m3M from the south bridge supports.

Poll a' Ghamhna, south of Eilean a' Ghamhna, one mile west of Kylesku is rather deep until close inshore, and the head of the bay dries off ½ cable.

A shoal spit extends ½ cable south from the southeast point of the island.

Kylestrome A pool north of Garbh Eilean on the north side of Kylesku is entered by a narrow channel northeast of Garbh Eilean across which runs a power cable with headroom of 15m.

Reefs extend more than halfway across the entrance channel from the north side leaving a passage perhaps no more than 20m wide; keep close to the southwest shore at the point where the channel narrows.

North Ferry Bay, north of Eilean na Rainich, is entered by the east and north sides of that island.

Drying and submerged rocks extend one cable from the north shore of the inlet and there are some fishing boat moorings.

Camas na Cusgaig (South Ferry Bay), south of the east point of the narrows, has several moorings in it.

A concrete fishing jetty stands at the northwest side of the head of the inlet.

A drying rock lies ¼ cable offshore at the north side of the entrance and although this sounds close enough to the shore, it can catch a stranger coming round the corner.

The bottom is very foul with old moorings, and a tripping line is strongly recommended. The concrete fishing pier although empty in the middle of the day is in constant use by local fishing boats and should not be used by visiting yachts other than for a short visit, for example for watering. Dinghy steps at the southwest corner of the pier.

Lights

2F.G(vert) are shown at the jetty.

Supplies

Post Office, telephone, hotel. Petrol and diesel at hotel by south ferry slip, water at jetty.

Lochs Glendhu and Glencoul

Two miles east of Kylesku the loch divides into two parts: Loch Glendhu to the east and Loch Glencoul to the southeast.

Loch Glendhu is clean with moderate depths at the head. Loch Glencoul has several hazards.

In its outer part the northeast shore is clean but, on the southwest side, a drying rock lies ¼ cable east of Eilean a Choin a' Chreige, the island furthest from the shore.

Another rock which dries 0·3m lies two cables southeast of the same island.

Loch Beag A narrow passage leads southwest of a group of islands, of which the largest is Eilean Ard, to Loch Beag.

A drying reef extends northeast from Eilean an Tuim at the west side of the narrows; hold towards the island north of Eilean Ard and then keep midway between the next island and the south shore.

A drying rock, which does not appear on some charts, lies south of the east end of this island.

The holding is very poor in deep soft silt, and strong williwaws slam down from all directions in winds above Force 5.

Good holding can be found between the 5–10m contours about one cable north of Eilean Ard.

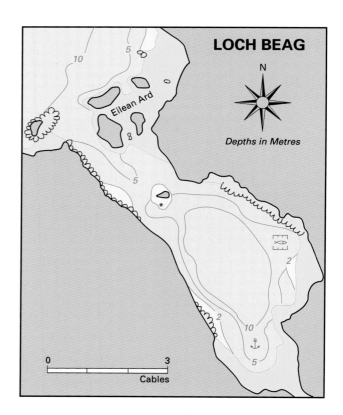

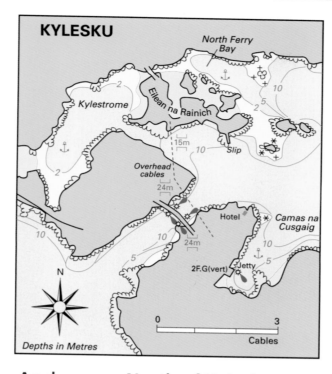

KYLESKU

North Ferry Bay

Kylestrome

Eilean na Rainich

Slip

Overhead cables

24m

Hotel

Camas na Cusgaig

24m

Jetty

2F.G(vert)

N

0   3

Cables

Depths in Metres

Anchorages North of Kylesku

Calbha Bay, 58°17′N 5°07′·5W, east of Calbha Mor, has fish cages along its west shore. Should these later be moved to the east side (fish cages are moved around to find cleaner water), care will be needed to avoid a reef which dries 3·1m extending about one cable from the west side.

Badcall Bay

58°19′N 5°09′W

A well-sheltered anchorage behind a dense group of islands on the east side of Eddrachillis Bay. A large number of fish cages lies on the southeast side of the bay.

Tides

Constant +0005 Ullapool (−0415 Dover)

Height in metres

MHWS	MHWN	MTL	MLWN	MLWS
4·5	3·4	2·6	1·6	0·9

Approach

From south, a possible hazard is a rock which dries 0·9m one cable south of Eilean na Bearachd.

South Channel lies east of Eilean na Bearachd, and west of Sgeir an Tairbh which is 1m high. At the northeast end of Eilean na Bearachd keep in mid-channel as reefs and drying rocks extend from either side.

Continue north for two cables until past a rock 0·9m high to starboard, and then head northeast.

Main Channel leads north of Ceannamhor and Eilean na Bearachd.

A submerged rock lies a cable north of Ceannamhor at a depth of 1·8m, and a rock which dries 0·3m lies ¼ cable south of Eilean Garbh.

From north, pass between Glas Leac and Eilean Garbh and enter by Main Channel.

Kylesku Bridge from south, with Camas na Cusgaig in the foreground

Badcall Islands with Ceannamhor at bottom left

Badcall Bay

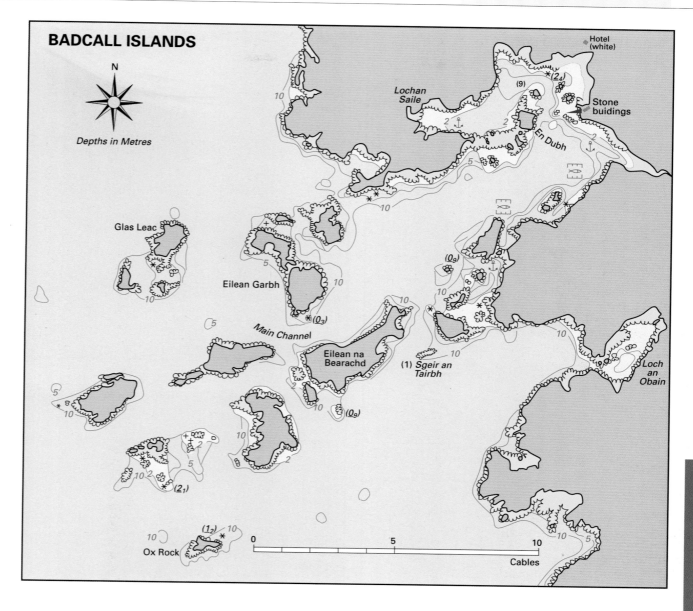

BADCALL ISLANDS

N

Depths in Metres

Hotel (white)

Lochan Saile

Stone buildings

En Dubh

Glas Leac

Eilean Garbh

(0₃)

Main Channel

Eilean na Bearachd

(0₉)

(1) Sgeir an Tairbh

Loch an Obain

(2₁)

(1₂)

Ox Rock

0   5   10

Cables

Lochan Saile on the north side of Badcall Bay is sheltered by islands and drying reefs. The bottom consists of soft mud and care should be taken that the anchor is well dug in.

To enter from Badcall Bay pass ¼ – ½ cable east of Eilean Dubh to avoid reefs extending east from the island, as well as drying and submerged rocks on the east side of the passage.

Pass east and north of the 9m islet north of Eilean Dubh and anchor in the western part of the bay.

Supplies

Water at slip on the east side of the passage to Lochan Saile. Hotel in the northeast corner, otherwise none (but *see Scourie*).

Scourie

58°21′N 5°10′W

This is the only source of stores between Lochinver and Kinlochbervie, apart from a small shop at Drumbeg. Scourie Bay is completely exposed, with several submerged and drying rocks in the entrance. If in doubt, go shopping by land from Badcall, about three miles by road.

Supplies

Shop, Post Office, telephone, hotel. Petrol, diesel and *Calor Gas* at garage.

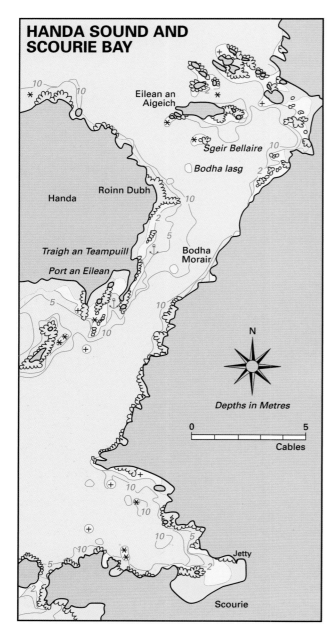

HANDA SOUND AND
SCOURIE BAY

Eilean an
Aigeich

Sgeir Bellaire

Bodha Iasg

Roinn Dubh

Handa

Traigh an Teampuill

Bodha
Morair

Port an Eilean

N

Depths in Metres

0 ———————— 5
Cables

Jetty

Scourie

Scourie

Port an Eilean, Handa, from west

Handa, Loch Laxford and Loch Inchard

Charts
2503 (1:25,000)
OS Landranger map 9

Handa Sound

58°23′N 5°10′W

Handa Island is an RSPB reserve with a resident warden.

Tides

Tidal streams in the sound run at up to 3kns.
The north-going stream begins −0405 Ullapool (+0400 Dover)
The south-going stream begins +0220 Ullapool (−0200 Dover)

Dangers and marks

Bodha Morair, in mid-channel in Handa Sound at a depth of 1·8m, causes heavy overfalls.

At the north end of the sound a drying reef extends one cable from Roinn Dubh on Handa, and Bodha Iasg lies in mid-channel at a depth of 1·6m.

Sgeir Bellaire, 1m high, lies on the northeast side of the passage, one cable south of Eilean an Aigeich, the largest and highest island in the north channel.

Occasional anchorages

Traigh an Teampuill on the east side of Handa, as close inshore as depth allows.

Port an Eilean at the southeast of the island. Approach from south-southwest; there are no clearing marks for the rocks on either side of the entrance.

Loch Laxford

58°25'N 5°07'W

Much of the land around the loch is bare reddish-coloured rock, with a little heather growing on peat in the hollows. The shores are broken and indented to an extraordinary extent and many anchorages can be found with the large-scale chart, although several of them contain fish cages.

Tides

Streams in the loch are insignificant.
Constant +0015 Ullapool (−0405 Dover)
Height in metres

MHWS	MHWN	MTL	MLWN	MLWS
4·9	3·5	2·8	1·9	0·7

Directions

The entrance, two miles northeast of Handa, is clean and straightforward, as is the fairway.

There are no lights and no supplies are available nearer than Scourie, which is about five miles by road from Foindle.

Anchorages

Crow Harbour (Fanagmore), 58°24'N 5°07'W, is the first anchorage on the south side on entering the loch.

Pass north and east of Eilean Ard (marked only '69' on chart *1785*), the largest and highest island in the loch, although even with only the small-scale chart it would be possible to cautiously thread a way through among the outer islands.

The principal hazard here is a drying rock one cable southwest of Sgeir Iosal which is 3½ cables west-northwest of Eilean Ard.

Although there is an extensive fish farm in the anchorage swinging room can still be found. Anchor on the west side, off the jetty.

Foindle Bay, 58°23'·8N 5°05'W, Bagh na Fionndalach Moire on the chart, about a mile east-southeast of Crow Harbour, is rather deep and the sides shelve steeply.

Enter by the north and east side of Eilean a Mhadaidh.

Weaver's Bay, 58°23'N 5°04'W, nearly a mile southeast of Foindle Bay, provides the best shelter in moderate depths of any bay on the south side of the loch.

Nearest supplies are at Scourie.

Loch a' Chadh-fi, 58°24'·5N 5°04'W, on the northeast side of the loch is entered by the east side of Eilean an Eireannaich (61m).

A rock which dries 2·8m lies ½ cable from the southeast shore three cables within the loch.

Eilean a' Chadh-fi lies in mid-channel about ¾ mile inside the loch. The deeper and broader channel is west and north of the island, but the west side of the loch is full of fish cages and moorings.

Hazards north of the island are avoided by keeping ½ cable off its shore.

Anchor north of the island, or anywhere in the upper part of the loch, but the head is shoal for about ¼ mile.

Several other anchorages may be found in Loch Laxford with the large-scale chart.

| Spenue | Ru Ruag | Fonnbhein | Arkle | Stack of Laxford |

Loch Laxford. Crow Harbour from south

Loch Inchard

58°27'·5N 5°05'W

Tides

Constant +0020 Ullapool (−0400 Dover)
Height in metres

MHWS	MHWN	MTL	MLWN	MLWS
4·9	3·6	2·8	1·9	0·7

Dangers and marks

Dubh Sgeirean is a group of islands about a mile offshore between Loch Laxford and Loch Inchard with a channel ½ mile wide between them and Sgeirean Cruaidhe nearer the shore.

Whale Back, which dries 3·8m southwest of Dubh Sgeirean is usually breaking.

Sgeir Geinn, 1½ cables west of the most southerly of Sgeirean Cruaidhe is awash at HW.

The most northerly of Sgeirean Cruaidhe is 8m high, which is not clear from chart *1785*, and Sgeir an Daimh, 3m high, lies three cables northwest of it.

The passage inshore of Dubh Sgeirean and east of Sgeir an Daimh can usually be taken.

Glas Leac, two islets at the south side of the entrance to Loch Inchard joined at low water, have a clear deep passage more than ½ cable wide inshore of them, but 3m patches 1½ cables southwest of them might cause a bad breaking sea if much swell is running.

Eilean an Roin Beag, two miles northwest of the mouth of Loch Inchard, is the most southwesterly point of land northwest of the approach to the loch.

Bodha Roin, nearly a cable southwest of the island, dries 0·7m.

Kinsale Rock (Bodha Ceann na Saile), four cables within the entrance just south of mid-channel at a depth of 3m, breaks if a swell is running. The southern extremity of the north shore of the loch in line with the south shore of Loch Sheigra ahead 098° leads north of Kinsale Rock.

Lights

Rubha na Leacaig on the north side of the entrance
Fl(2)10s30m8M

Cape Wrath lighthouse, Fl(4)30s122m24M, is obscured east of about 025°, or the line of the coast north of Eilean an Roin Beag

Loch Bervie (Kinlochbervie)

58°27′·5N 5°03′W

The third-largest fishing harbour in Scotland by volume of fish landed, this is often too busy for a visiting yacht to find space although a pontoon has been provided for small craft in the north-northeast corner.

Pontoons are provided for visiting yachts on the west side, south of the ice tower.

The entrance is dredged between drying banks marked by light beacons, but take note of the spit on the east side extending west, well north of the beacon on that side.

A fluorescent yellow framework tower stands at the head of the harbour, with daylight intensity directional lights, the white sector bearing 327° leads into the harbour.

A beacon on the south shore of Loch Inchard, *Creag Mhor*, provides a white light sector 1° wide bearing 147°.

Kinlochbervie Harbour ☎ 01971 521235

Lights

Leading lights Dir.WRG.16m9M
No. 1 beacon Fl.R.4s
No. 2 beacon Q.R
No. 3 beacon Fl.G.4s
Creag Mhor, Oc.WRG.2·8s

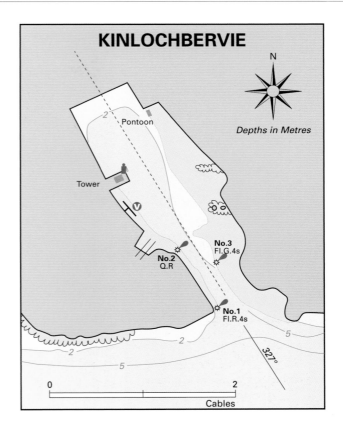

KINLOCHBERVIE

Depths in Metres

Pontoon

Tower

No.3 Fl.G.4s

No.2 Q.R

No.1 Fl.R.4s

327°

Cables

Kinlochbervie

Kinlochbervie entrance at low water

Radio
VHF Ch 14 (all times).
☎ 01971 521235, *Mobile* 07901 514350.

Services and supplies
Shop (uphill from the harbour), Post Office, telephone, hotel.

Showers may be available at the Royal National Mission to Deep Sea Fishermen (not weekends).

Petrol at garage. Diesel and water at quay, *Calor Gas.*

Fishermen's chandlery, mechanical, electronic, hull repairs.

Minor anchorages
Mol Bhain (Camas Blair) on the south shore ½ mile southwest of the entrance to Loch Bervie.

Anchor ½ cable off the southwest shore; subject to swell and wash from passing traffic (there may be a fish farm by now).

Loch Sheigra, 58°27'N 5°01'W, one mile east of Loch Bervie, is mostly shoal and drying, but has a depth of 2m one cable within the entrance.

Stores at Badcall on the north shore.

Achriesgill Bay, one mile further southeast, dries at the head and the bottom drops steeply to more than 15m.

Rhiconich, 58°26'N 5°00'W, at the head of the loch. The water in the middle is shoal for about ½ mile from the head of the loch, but deeper on either side. Hotel, Post Office, telephone, garage.

Anchorages north of Loch Inchard
Loch Clash, 58°27'·7N 5°04'W, is open to the west and used by fishing boats for landing their catches but, in quiet weather, is an alternative to entering Loch Bervie for stores.

Coastal passage to Cape Wrath
Cape Wrath is 10 miles from Eilean an Roin Beag and there is no secure shelter eastward nearer than Loch Eriboll, a further 14 miles.

Dangers and marks
Eilean an Roin Beag – Dubh Sgeir, 10m high, lies ½ mile north of Eilean an Roin Beag and rocks above water and drying lie between Dubh Sgeir and the coast ½ mile north-northeast.

Am Balg, 44m high, lies a mile offshore four miles north of Eilean an Roin Beag with drying rocks up to two cables from it.

Waypoint one mile west of Am Balg, 57°33'N 5°09'W

Duslic Rock, which dries 3·4m, lies seven cables north-northeast of Cape Wrath. Am Balg just open northwest of Cape Wrath 215° leads west of Duslic Rock.

Tides
Tidal streams reach 1¾kns at springs.

The north-going stream begins –0110 Ullapool (–0530 Dover).

The south-going stream begins +0505 Ullapool (+0045 Dover).

It is noted that a south-going eddy runs ½–¾ miles offshore during the north-going tide.

Appendix

I. Charts and other publications

Imray charts

Imray's C65, C66 and C67, at a scale of about 1:150,000, cover the waters referred to in this volume. They are available at most chandlers and from the Clyde Cruising Club, usually folded, but for any boat which has a large enough chart table it is better to order a flat copy.

Imray chart pack 2800, covers Crinan to Fort William and the Sound of Mull
www.imray.com

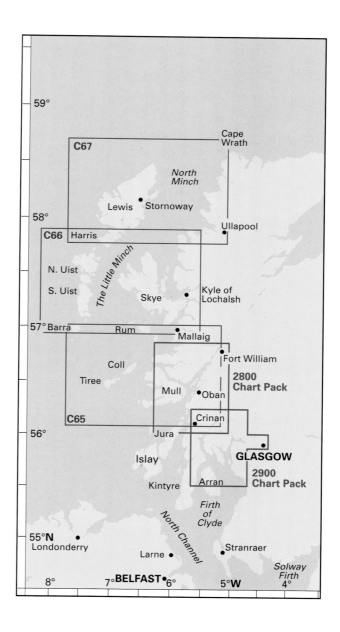

UKHO and OS

A general chart for the whole west coast of Scotland is Admiralty chart 2635 at a scale of 1:500,000. The following Admiralty charts relate to the waters covered by this volume. Some of these are essential and, the more you have, the less your pilotage will be fraught with anxiety. The relevant Ordnance Survey maps are also listed. OSL = Landranger. OSE = Explorer.

Chart	Title – areas in Chapters I and II	Scale
2207	Ardnamurchan to Sound of Sleat	1:50,000
2208	Mallaig to Canna Harbour	1:50,000
OSL39	Rhum, Eigg and Muck	1:50,000
OSL40	Mallaig and Glenfinnan	1:50,000
OSE390	Moidart, Sunart and Loch Shiel	1:25,000
OSE398	Loch Morar and Mallaig	1:25,000
OSE397	Rùm, Eigg, Muck, Canna and Sanday	1:25,000

Chart	Title – areas in Chapter III	Scale
2208	Mallaig to Canna Harbour	1:50,000
1795	The Little Minch	1:100,000
2533	Lochs Dunvegan and Snizort	1:25,000
OSL32	South Skye	1:50,000
OSL23	North Skye	1:50,000
OSE390	Moidart, Sunart and Loch Shiel	1:25,000
OSE398	Loch Morar & Mallaig	1:25,000
OSE407	Skye – Dunvegan	1:25,000
OSE409	Raasay, Rona and Scalpay	1:25,000
OSE410	Skye - Portree and Bracadale	1:25,000
OSE411	Skye – Cuillin Hills, Soay	1:25,000

Chart	Title – areas in Chapter IV	Scale
2208	Mallaig to Canna Harbour	1:50,000
2209	Inner Sound	1:50,000
2541	Lochs Nevis, Hourn and Duich	1:25,000
2540	Loch Alsh	1:25,000
OSL33	Lochalsh, Glen Shiel & Loch Hourn	1:50,000
OSE412	Skye – Sleat Broadford, Kyleakin & Armadale	1:25,000
OS 413	Knoydart, Loch Hourn & Loch Duich	1:25,000

Chart	Title – areas in Chapter V	Scale
2209	Inner Sound	1:50,000
2210	Approaches to Inner Sound	1:50,000
2534	Plans in the Inner Sound	1:25,000
2528	Loch Carron and Loch Gairloch	1:25,000
2498	Inner Sound, Southern Part	1:25,000
2479	Inner Sound, Middle Part	1:18,000
2480	Inner Sound, Northern Part	1:25,000
OSL33	Lochalsh, Glen Shiel & Loch Hourn	1:50,000
OSL24	Raasay and Applecross	1:50,000
OSE 428	Kyle of Lochalsh, Plockton & Applecross	1:25,000
OSE433	Torridon – Beinn Eighe and Liathach	1:25,000
OSE434	Gairloch and Loch Ewe	1:25,000

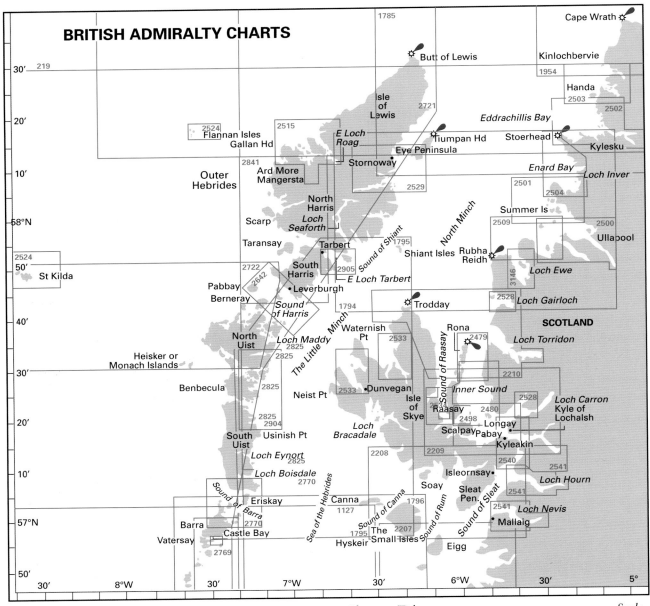

BRITISH ADMIRALTY CHARTS

Chart	Title – areas in Chapters VI to VIII	Scale
1785	North Minch, Northern Part	1:100,000
1794	North Minch, Southern Part	1:100,000
2509	Rubha Reidh to Cailleach Head	1:25,000
2500	Loch Broom and Approaches	1:25,000
2501	Summer Isles	1:26,000
2502	Eddrachillis Bay	1:25,150
2503	Lochs Laxford and Inchard	1:25,000
2504	Approaches to Loch Inver	1:25,000
3146	Loch Ewe	1:12,500
OSL19	Gairloch and Ullapool	1:50,000
OSL15	Loch Assynt	1:50,000
OSL9	Cape Wrath	1:50,000
OSE409	Raasay, Rona and Scalpay	1:25,000
OSE412	Skye – Sleat Broadford, Kyleakin and Armadale	1:25,000
OSE429	Glen Carron and West Monar	1:25,000
OSE433	Torridon – Beinn Eighe and Liathach	1:25,000
OSE434	Gairloch and Loch Ewe	1:25,000
OSE435	An Teallach and Slioch	1:25 000

Chart	Title	Scale
OSE442	Assynt and Lochinver: Kylesku and Inchnadamph	1:25,000
OSE445	Foinaven, Arkle, Kylesku & Scourie	1:25,000
OSE446	Durness and Cape Wrath: Kinlochbervie & Rhiconich	1:25,000

OS Explorer at 1:25,000 are occasionally useful where there is no Admiralty chart at a sufficiently large scale. An index sheet of all OS maps is available from larger bookshops and from Ordnance Survey, Romsey Road, Southampton SO16 4GU ☎ 08456 050505 www.ordnancesurvey.co.uk

There are Admiralty chart agents throughout Britain, and in most other countries. Chart agents on the West Coast are:

Kelvin Hughes, 22 St Luke's Business Estate, 22 St Luke's Place, Glasgow G5 0TS ☎ 0141 429 6462

Johnston Brothers, Mallaig ☎ 01687 462215

Imray, Laurie, Norie & Wilson Ltd are Admiralty chart agents and will supply charts by post from Wych House, The Broadway, St Ives, Huntingdon, Cambridgeshire PE27 5BT ☎ 01480 462114, *Fax* 01480 496109 www.imray.com

Some charts which have long been discontinued provide much more detail, at a larger scale, than any now published for the same area. All older charts, particularly the fine Victorian engravings, show more detail inshore and on land than the current publications, although they may be less accurate.

Old charts should only be used to supplement current ones, not as a substitute for them. The following old charts in particular may be found useful:

531 Loch Moidart (1:7,900)
2817 Loch na Ceall (1:10,700)
2638 Loch Torridon (1:25,000)

Photocopies of old charts – of editions not less than 50 years old, for copyright reasons – may be obtained from:
National Library of Scotland Map Room Annexe, 33 Salisbury Place, Edinburgh EH9 1SL ☎ 0131 623 3970 *Email* maps@nls.uk

Many early charts can be viewed on screen at www.nls.uk

Current charts show less detail ashore than older charts, and Ordnance Survey maps at a scale of 1:25,000 (Explorer) and 1:50,000 (Landranger) help to fill in the picture.

The Clyde Cruising Club Sailing Directions and Anchorages are available from the CCC at Suite 101, The Pentagon Centre, Washington St, Glasgow G3 8AZ ☎ 0141 221 2774 *Fax* 0141 221 2775.

The Admiralty *West Coast of Scotland Pilot* (NP 66) is now published every three years or so without regular Supplements, but any important corrections are published in *Weekly Notices to Mariners*.

Admiralty Notices to Mariners, both weekly and quarterly Small Craft Editions are available on the internet at www.ukho.gov.uk

The Admiralty *Tidal stream atlas for the North Coast of Ireland and West Coast of Scotland* (NP 218) is very useful.

Tide tables are essential, preferably for Ullapool giving heights of each high and low water.

Almanacs

The Cruising Almanac (Cruising Association and Imray).

Pilotage books

Ardnamurchan to Cape Wrath Sailing Directions Clyde Cruising Club.

General books

The Scottish Islands, by Hamish Haswell Smith, is an extremely useful general guide, published by Canongate.

Exploring Scotland's Heritage – The Highlands, Joanna Close-Brooks (HMSO 1986).

The Islands of Scotland including Skye, Scottish Mountaineering Club, 1989 (for climbers and hillwalkers).

Cruising Scotland Clyde Cruising Club, 2010.

Lochs and Lights: The west coast of mainland Scotland by Patrick Roach and Gordon Buchanan. Imray.

Mariners are invited to contact the Navigation Section, Northern Lighthouse Board. *Email* navigation@nlb.org.uk, to comment on any aspect of the Aids to Navigation Service, or on hazards to navigation around our coasts.

Kayaks at Hallaig

II. Glossary of Gaelic words which commonly appear in place names

Many varieties of spelling are found, so it is as well to search for possible alternatives; variations of the same word are listed together but usually at least have the same initial letter. Many words beginning with a consonant take an 'h' after the initial letter in certain cases; notably in adjectives the genitive and the feminine gender and genitive cases of nouns, so that most of the words below could have an 'h' as the second letter.

There is no possibility of guiding the reader on pronunciation except to say that consonants followed by an 'h' are not often pronounced, and that 'mh' and 'bh' at the beginning of a word are pronounced as (and of course in anglicised versions often spelt with) a 'v'. *Mhor* is pronounced – approximately – *vore*; *claidheamh* is something like *clayeh*, and *bogha* is *bo'a*.

Some names, particularly those of islands ending in 'a' or 'ay', are of Norse origin. Anyone at all familiar with French and Latin will see correspondences there, for example Caisteil – also Eaglais and Teampuill.

Many words are compounds made up of several often quite common parts, frequently linked by *na/nam/nan*. The following are the most usual forms of words which commonly occur in Gaelic place names. They often set out to describe the physical features and so give some clues to identification. Some of them occur almost everywhere; most lochs have a Sgeir More and an Eilean Dubh, or vice versa.

Gaelic	English
a, am, an, an t-	the
abhainn (avon)	river
acairseid	harbour (acair = anchor)
achadh (ach, auch)	field
allt	stream, burn
ard, aird	promontory
aros	house
ba	cattle
bairneach	limpet
bagh ('bay')	bay
ban	white, pale; female (ban-righ = queen); as noun: woman
bealach	narrow passage
beg, beag, beaga	small
ben, beinn	mountain
beul (bel)	mouth of (belnahua = mouth of the cave)
bodach	old man
bogha (bo')	a detached rock, usually one which uncovers
breac	speckled (as noun: trout)
buachaille	shepherd
buidhe (bhuidhe, buie)	yellow (also: pleasing)
bun	mouth of a river
cailleach	old woman
caisteil	castle
camas	bay
caol (a' chaolais)	narrow passage (kyle)

Gaelic	English
caorach	sheep
ceall, cille (kil...)	monastic cell, church
ceann (kin...)	head
clachan	usually a group of houses (clach = stone)
claidheamh	sword (hence 'claymore' = great sword)
cnoc (knock)	rounded hill
coire (corrie)	cauldron, hollow among hills, whirlpool
craobh	tree
creag	cliff, rock (crag)
darroch	oak tree
dearg ('jerrig')	red
deas	south
dobhran	otter
donn	brown (dun)
druim	ridge
dubh (dhu)	black, dark, (disastrous)
dun, duin	fortified place, usually prehistoric
each	horse
ear	east
eilean (or eileach)	island
fada	long
fir, fear	man
fraoch, fraoich	heather
garbh	rough
geal	white
gille	boy
glas	grey (sometimes green)
gobhar (gour)	goat (gabhar = she-goat)
gorm	blue
gamhna	stirk, year-old calf
iar	west (easily confused with Ear)
iolair	eagle
keills, kells	church
kin... (ceann)	head of
liath	grey
mara	sea
meadhonach	middle-sized
meall	lump, knob
mor (more, mhor, vore)	large, great (often only relative)
muc, muck	pig (often a sea-pig = porpoise or a whale)
na, na h-, nam, nan of	(the)naomh (nave, neave) holy, saint
...nish (ness)	point of land
poll, puill	pool
righ ('ree')	king
ron, roin	seal
ruadh, rudha	red, reddish
rubha (rhu)	point of land, promontory
sailean	creek
sgeir, sgeirean (skerry)	rock, above water or covering
sron	nose (as a headland)
sruth	stream, current
tigh	house
tober	well
traigh	beach
tuath (or tuadh)	north
uamh	cave

III. Submarine exercise areas

SUBFACTS are available through Faslane Operations Room (FOSNNI) ☎ 01436 674321 *Ext.* 3206 / 6778.

SUBFACTS may also be obtained using the Faslane Fisherman's Hotline ☎ 01436 677201

Transmissions of:
0121	Belfast CG
0088	Cullercoats (GCC)
0070	Clyde
0072	Clyde CG
0075	Oban CG
0065	Portpatrick (GPK)
0079	Stornoway CG

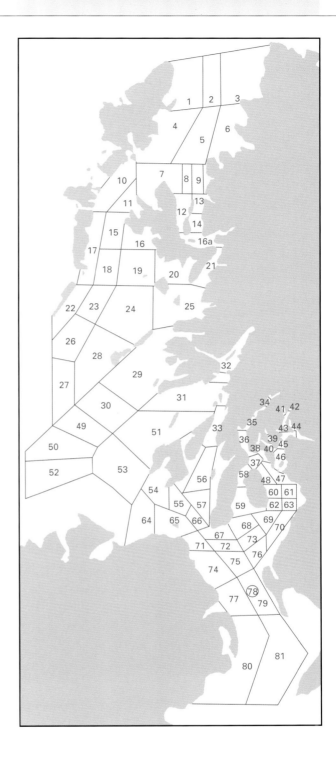

1.	Tiumpan X5816	41.	Goil X5604
2.	Minch North X5817	42.	Long X5606
3.	Stoer X5818	43.	Cove X5605
4.	Shiant X5815	44.	Gareloch X5620
5.	Minch South X5814	45.	Rosneath X5506
6.	Ewe X5813	46.	Cumbrae X5507
7.	Trodday X5715	47.	Garroch X5508
8.	Rona West X5716	48.	Laggan X5509
9.	Rona North X5717	49.	Blackstone X5542
10.	Lochmaddy X5713	50.	Place X5541
11.	Dunvegan X5714	51.	Colonsay X5543
12.	Portree X5720	52.	Boyle X5540
13.	Rona South X5718	53.	Orsay X5539
14.	Raasay X5719	54.	Islay X5538
15.	Neist X5711	55.	Otter X5535
16.	Bracadale X5709	56.	Gigha X5534
16A	Crowlin X5705	57.	Earadale X5533
17.	Ushenish X5712	58.	Lochranza X5515
18.	Hebrides North X5710	59.	Davaar X5514
19.	Canna X5708	60.	Brodick X5510
20.	Rhum X5707	61.	Irvine X5511
21.	Sleat X5706	62.	Lamlash X5513
22.	Barra X5633	63.	Ayr X5512
23.	Hebrides Central X5632	64.	Skerries X5537
24.	Hawes X5635	65.	Rathlin X5536
25.	Eigg X5636	66.	Kintyre X5531
26.	Hebrides South X5631	67.	Sanda X5530
27.	Ford X5630	68.	Stafnish X5523
28.	Tiree X5634	69.	Pladda X5522
29.	Staffa X5627	70.	Turnberry X5521
30.	Mackenzie X5626	71.	Torr X5528
31.	Mull X5628	72.	Mermaid X5529
32.	Linnhe X5624	73.	Ailsa X5524
33.	Jura Sound X5623	74.	Maiden X5529
34.	Fyne X5603	75.	Corsewall X5526
35.	Minard X5602	76.	Ballantrae X5525
36.	Tarbert X5517	77.	Magee X5407
37.	Skipness X5516	78.	Londonderry X5401
38.	West Kyle X5518	79.	Beaufort X5408
39.	Striven X5520	80.	Ardglass X5402
40.	East Kyle X5519	81.	Peel X5403

IV. Quick reference table of provisions, services and supplies

1	Water	A	Alongside, by hose
		T	Tap on jetty or quay
		N	Nearby tap
2	Shop	S	Several, or supermarket
		L	Local, well stocked village store
		B	Basic
3	Diesel	A	Alongside, by hose
		M	Marine diesel, near
		G	Garage
4	Petrol	P	(usually needs to be carried some distance)
5	Calor Gas	C	
6	Repairs	H	Hull
		M	Marine engine
		E	Electronics (engineer may need to come from a distance)

7	Chandlery	Y	Yacht
		F	Fishermen's chandlery
		I	Ironmonger, hardware store, which may be better than nothing
8	Visitors' moorings	V	(including those provided by hotel for customers)
		P	Pontoon
9	Conveniences	R	Restaurant
		B	Bar
		S	Showers
10	Bank	£	
11	Rubbish disposal	D	

Page	Place	1	2	3	4	5	6	7	8	9	10	11
20	Glenuig		L½							RB		
30	Arisaig harbour	A	S	M	P	G		(F)	V	RB		
31	Morar		L	G	P					RB		
32	Mallaig	A	S	D	P	C	HME	YF		RB	£	D
38	Eigg		L			C				CS		
41	Rum	L										
52	Loch Beg		L							RB		
52	Portnalong		Ly							RB		
53	Carbost	N	L						V	RB		
56	Dunvegan		S	G	P	C	F	I	V	RBS		D
57	Stein		B				ME	Y	V	RBS		
57	Edinbane		S	G	P					RB		
58	Uig	T	L	G	P		HME			RB		
62	Inverie		L						V	RB		
65	Doune Bay	A		A			HM		V	RS		
65	Armadale	T	L	M			HM		V	RB		D
68	Isleornsay	N	B		P					RB		
71	Glenelg		L		P	C				RB		
73	Dornie		S		P	C				RB		
74	Balmacara		L			C				RB		
74	Kyle Akin	T	S	G	P	C			VP	RBS		D
76	Kyle of Lochalsh	A	S	G	P	C	E	1(Y)	P	RBS	£	D
80	Ardarroch		L	G	P							
80	Plockton	(A)	G	S	M	C				RBS		
82	Lochcarron		S	G	P	C		I		RB		D
87	Poll Creadha		B		P							
90	Shieldaig		S			C				RB		D
91	Torridon		L							RB		
91	Badachro	A	L	A				Y	V	RBS		D
93	Gairloch	A	S1	G1	P1	C	M		P	RB	£	D
94	Broadford		S	G	P					RB		
99	Portree	A	S	M	P	C	M	FI	V	RB	£	D
105	Staffin		L									
108	Aultbea	T	S		P	C	(ME)			RB		
108	Poolewe		L	G	P	C				RB		
109	Ullapool	A	S	A	P	C	ME	YFI		RB	£	D
113	Achiltibuie		S							RB		
116	Loch Inver	A	S	A	AP	C		F		RB		D
118	Drumbeg	T	B							RB		
124	Kylesku	T	L	A	P					RB		
127	Scourie		L		PG	C				RB		
131	Kinlochbervie	A	S	A	P	C	HME	F		RBS		D

Notes
Figures following reference letter indicate the distance in miles from the landing place.
Caley Marine at Inverness ☎ 01463 236539 operates a mobile repair service.

Index